A Streetcar Named Desire

by Tennessee Williams

Nicola Onyett

Series Editors:
Nicola Onyett and Luke McBratney

HODDER
EDUCATION
AN HACHETTE UK COMPANY

The publisher would like to thank the following for permission to reproduce copyright material:

Acknowledgements:

Tennessee Williams: from *A Streetcar Named Desire* (Penguin, 2009); **p.15: Harold Arlen, E. Y. Harburg and Billy Rose:** from 'It's Only a Paper Moon' Words by E Y Harburg and Billy Rose Music by Harold Arlen, © 1933 WB Music Corp, Glocca Morra Music Corp and Shapiro Bernstein & Co Inc (66.66%) Warner/Chappell North America Ltd, London, W8 5DA and (33.34%) Shapiro Bernstein & Co Limited, New York, NY 10022-5718, USA Reproduced by permission of Faber Music Ltd All Rights; **p.18: Ben Hecht:** taken from 'Gone With the Wind' (MGM, 1939); **p.21: Primo Levi:** from *Other People's Trades* (Abacus, 1999); **pp.21,36,52,69,70,74,77,80,82: Matthew C. Roudané:** from *The Cambridge Companion to Tennessee Williams* (Cambridge University Press, 1997), reproduced by permission of Cambridge University Press; **pp.23,36,65: Alycia Smith-Howard and Greta Heintzelman:** from *Critical Companion to Tennessee Williams: A Literary Reference to His Life and Work* (Checkmark Books, 2005), reproduced by permission of the publisher; **p.30: Tennessee Williams:** from *The Glass Menagerie* (Penguin, 2009); **p.32: Aristotle:** From Aristotle's theory on tragedy (330BC); **p.33: Tennessee Williams:** from *Memoirs* (Penguin Classics, 2007); **pp.33,39: Robert C. Small:** from *A Teacher's Guide to the Signet edition of Tennessee Williams' 'A Streetcar Named Desire'* (Penguin Putnam, 2004); **pp.38,61,68,70,71: Tennessee Williams:** from *Cat on a Hot Tin Roof* (Penguin Classics, 2009); **pp.53,56–7,60: Tennessee Williams:** from *Notebooks* (Yale University Press, 2007); **p.61: Ted Hughes:** from 'Ted Hughes' from *The Guardian* (The Guardian, 22nd July 2008); **p.61: Henry Luce:** from 'American Century' from *Time Magazine* (Time Magazine, 17th February 1941); **p.62:** From the *Declaration of Independence* (4th July 1776); **p.62: Emma Lazarus:** from 'The New Colossus' (1883); **p.62: James Truslow Adams:** from *The Epic of America* (Simon Publications, 2001); **pp.66,70: Elia Kazan:** discussing Blanche and Tennessee Williams; **p.67: Molly Haskell:** from *Frankly, My Dear: 'Gone with the Wind' Revisited* (Yale University Press, 2010), reproduced by permission of the publisher; **p.69: Hart Crane:** from 'The Broken Tower' (1932); **p.68: Flannery O'Connor:** from *Everything That Rises Must Converge* (Farrar, Straus and Giroux, 1996); **pp.72–3: John Russell Taylor:** from *Vivien Leigh* (H.Hamilton, 1984); **p.78: Terry Eagleton:** from *Marxism and Literary Criticism* (Routledge, 1976), reproduced by permission of the publisher; **pp.78,79: Arthur Miller:** from 'Tragedy and the Common Man' from *The New York Times* (The New York Times, 27th February 1949), reproduced by permission of *The New York Times*; **pp.78,81: C.W.E Bigsby:** from *Modern American Drama 1945–2000* (Cambridge University Press, 2008), reproduced by permission of Cambridge University Press; **p.81: Arthur Miller:** from *Timebends: A Life* (Bloomsbury, 2012), reproduced by permission of The Wylie Agency; **p.82: Henry Hitchings:** from 'Rachel Weisz mesmerizes in magical Streetcar Named Desire' from *The Evening Standard* (The Evening Standard, 29th July 2009), reproduced by permission of *The Evening Standard*, www.standard.co.uk; **pp.82–3: Charles Spencer:** from 'A Streetcar Named Desire, Young Vic, review' from *The Telegraph* (The Telegraph, 29th July 2014), © Telegraph Media Group Limited 2014.

Every effort has been made to trace or contact all copyright holders, but if any have been inadvertently overlooked the Publishers will be pleased to make the necessary arrangements at the first opportunity.

Photo credits:

p.3 © ITV/REX; **p.5** © Carol M. Highsmith/Buyenlarge/Getty Images; **p.9** © Alastair Muir/REX; **p.14** © cineclassico / Alamy; **p.25** © The Washington Post - Getty Images; **p.35** © JP Jazz Archive/Redferns/Getty Images; **p.42** © Jerry Cooke/Pix Inc./The LIFE Images Collection/Getty Images; **p.50** © SNAP/REX; **p.59** © Popperfoto/Getty Images; **p.64** https://commons.wikimedia.org/wiki/File:Map_of_CSA_4.png - Public Domain; **p.66** © Michael Ochs/Corbis; **p.72** © SNAP/REX; **p.77** © ClassicStock / Alamy; **p.84** © Alastair Muir/REX

Although every effort has been made to ensure that website addresses are correct at time of going to press, Hodder Education cannot be held responsible for the content of any website mentioned. It is sometimes possible to find a relocated web page by typing in the address of the home page for a website in the URL window of your browser.

Orders: please contact Bookpoint Ltd, 130 Milton Park, Abingdon, Oxon OX14 4SB. Telephone: (44) 01235 827720. Fax: (44) 01235 400454. Lines are open 9.00–17.00, Monday to Saturday, with a 24-hour message answering service. Visit our website at www.hoddereducation.co.uk

© Nicola Onyett 2016

First published in 2016 by

Hodder Education
An Hachette UK Company,
Carmelite House, 50 Victoria Embankment
London EC4Y 0DZ

Impression number	5	4
Year	2020	2019

Cover photo (and throughout) © Elly - Fotolia

Typeset in 11/13pt Univers LT Std 47 Light Condensed by Integra Software Services Pvt. Ltd., Pondicherry, India

Printed in Dubai

A catalogue record for this title is available from the British Library

ISBN 9781471853739

Contents

Using this guide iv

Introduction vi

1   Synopsis 1

2   Scene summaries and commentaries 3

3   Themes 21

4   Characters 25

5   Writer's methods: form, structure and language 30

6   Contexts 59

7   Working with the text 85

    Assessment Objectives and skills 85

    Building skills 1: Structuring your writing 88

    Building skills 2: Analysing texts in detail 95

    Top ten quotations 101

    Taking it further 105

Using this guide

Why read this guide?

The purposes of this A-level Literature Guide are to enable you to organise your thoughts and responses to the text, deepen your understanding of key features and aspects and help you to address the particular requirements of examination questions and non-exam assessment tasks in order to obtain the best possible grade. It will also prove useful to those of you writing an NEA piece on the text as it provides a number of summaries, lists, analyses and references to help with the content and construction of the assignment.

Note that teachers and examiners are seeking above all else evidence of an *informed personal response to the text*. A guide such as this can help you to understand the text, form your own opinions, and suggest areas to think about, but it cannot replace your own ideas and responses as an informed and autonomous reader.

Page references in this guide refer to the Methuen student edition of *A Streetcar Named Desire* edited by Patricia Hern and Michael Hooper (2009). This edition has excellent introductory material and comprehensive notes. Where a publication is given in the 'Taking it further' section on pages 105–106, the author's surname and publication date only are cited after the first full reference.

How to make the most of this guide

You may find it useful to read sections of this guide when you need them, rather than reading it from start to finish. For example, you may find it helpful to read the 'Contexts' section before you start reading the text, or to read the 'Scene summaries and commentaries' section in conjunction with the text – whether to back up your first reading of it at school or college or to help you revise. The sections relating to the Assessment Objectives will be especially useful in the weeks leading up to the exam.

Key elements

This guide is designed to help you to raise your achievement in your examination response to *A Streetcar Named Desire*. It is intended for you to use throughout your AS/A-level English literature course. It will help you when you are studying the play for the first time and also during your revision.

The following features have been used throughout this guide to help you focus your understanding of the play:

Context

Context boxes give contextual evidence that relates directly to particular aspects of the text.

TASK

Tasks are short and focused. They allow you to engage directly with a particular aspect of the text.

CRITICAL VIEW

Critical view boxes highlight a particular critical viewpoint that is relevant to an aspect of the main text. This allows you to develop the higher-level skills needed to come up with your own interpretation of a text.

Build critical skills

Broaden your thinking about the text by answering the questions in the **Build critical skills** boxes. These help you to consider your own opinions in order to develop your skills of criticism and analysis.

Taking it further ▶

Taking it further boxes suggest and provide further background or illuminating parallels to the text.

Top ten quotation ◁ Top ten quotation

A cross-reference to Top ten quotations (see pages 101–104 of this guide), where each quotation is accompanied by a commentary that shows why it is important.

Introduction

A Streetcar Named Desire (1947) is one of the most celebrated and iconic American plays of the twentieth century. Cementing its author Tennessee Williams' place in the front rank of American writers and earning him the Pulitzer Prize for Drama, its contemporary cultural impact was immense. Along with his great contemporaries Eugene O'Neill and Arthur Miller, Williams is now considered one of the principal architects of the all-conquering American drama that dominated the twentieth century. Set in the vibrant, multicultural, working-class Vieux Carré Quarter of New Orleans, the play is firmly embedded within its specific post-World War II socio-cultural context; both intensely personal and highly political, its central characters, the fading Southern belle Blanche DuBois and the brash, second-generation Polish immigrant Stanley Kowalski, have been seen as representatives of the enormous culture clash between the gently declining Old South and the thrusting materialist and consumerist society which was threatening to overwhelm it.

The play's performance history is now semi-legendary. The original 1947 Broadway stage production of *A Streetcar Named Desire* directed by Elia Kazan made an instant legend of its leading man, the unknown 24-year-old Marlon Brando, while the 1949 London West End version directed by Laurence Olivier and starring his film star wife Vivien Leigh was received almost as enthusiastically. In 1951, the electrifying combination of Brando and Leigh as Stanley and Blanche contributed to one of the best Hollywood screen versions of a stage play ever made, again under the direction of Elia Kazan and with the full cooperation of Tennessee Williams. Marlon Brando's astonishing good looks and touchingly naïve vulnerability made his portrayal of the brutish working-class anti-hero Stanley Kowalski an iconic touchstone of American drama; indeed his performance both on stage and screen was a watershed moment in terms of its theatrical resonance. Brando's naturalistic and realistic 'Method' acting style, which seemed to highlight a side of Stanley that was less the violent, domestic tyrant and more the wary and vulnerable boy, served to hardwire the play into American popular culture; indeed it is hard to imagine many other classic literary works so widely known and instantly recognisable that fifty-odd years after they were first performed they can be parodied in a gloriously funny episode of *The Simpsons*. Even today, seven decades after it was written, *A Streetcar Named Desire* is frequently revived on stage to huge acclaim. In many ways, Tennessee Williams is the dramatists' dramatist, recognised by his fellow playwrights as one of the all-time greats. As Peter Shaffer has said of him, 'He was a born dramatist as few are ever born. Whatever he put on paper, superb or superfluous, glorious or gaudy, could not fail to be electrifyingly actable. He could not write a dull scene . . . Tennessee Williams will live as long as drama itself.'

Synopsis

Blanche DuBois, an English teacher from Laurel, Mississippi, arrives to stay with her sister and brother-in-law, Stella and Stanley Kowalski, in their cramped apartment in a lively multicultural working-class district of New Orleans. All is clearly not well; the sisters' childhood home, Belle Reve, has been mysteriously 'lost' and Blanche has left her job because of her bad nerves.

Blanche proves a troublesome guest; she hogs the bathroom, expects the pregnant Stella to fetch and carry for her and drinks Stanley's whisky on the sly even while criticising the Kowalskis' 'common' way of life. At first Stanley suspects Blanche has cheated Stella out of her share of the family inheritance, but it becomes clear that Belle Reve was repossessed after the family defaulted on a mortgage.

One evening Stanley and his friends play poker and Mitch, who lives with his sick mother, is attracted to Blanche. An ugly scene erupts which ends with Stanley hitting his pregnant wife. Although Stella runs upstairs to take refuge with her friend Eunice, when Stanley calls for her she returns. Despite everything, they are passionately in love.

As the hot summer wears on, Mitch and Blanche begin to date; she maintains a pose of genteel innocence which utterly charms him. She also describes her young husband's homosexuality and how her shocked reaction helped drive him to kill himself. Mitch's elderly mother is eager for him to find someone to be with after she dies and it seems these two lonely people might be able to comfort one another.

Meanwhile, however, Stanley has dug up the truth about Blanche's shady past in Laurel, which is a world away from the virginal act she has assumed for Mitch's benefit; her promiscuous behaviour was too much even for the Flamingo, the seedy low-rent hotel she called home, and she was evicted. Worse, she became involved with a 17-year-old student at her school; when the boy's father complained, she was instantly dismissed. Broke and homeless, Blanche was left with no one to turn to except Stella.

Stella is aghast when she finds that Stanley has told Mitch the truth about her sister, but he says he owed his old army buddy the truth. Mitch boycotts Blanche's birthday party on the afternoon of 15 September, while Stanley's 'gift' is a bus ticket back to Laurel. Another violent argument breaks out between the Kowalskis which ends abruptly when Stella goes into labour. Stanley takes her to the hospital and Blanche is left alone in the apartment.

Later the same evening Mitch arrives to see Blanche, who has been drinking heavily. She tells him the truth about her past, hoping they can still be together, but he tells her she is not fit to marry and makes a clumsy attempt to assault her. Blanche fights him off and he leaves at once.

Now teetering on the edge of madness, Blanche believes she is about to leave New Orleans for a Caribbean cruise with her old beau Shep Huntleigh. Stanley returns home and tells her Stella's baby will not be born until the morning. The tension between them finally explodes and although the frantic Blanche tries to defend herself with a broken bottle, Stanley disarms her easily and then rapes her.

Some weeks later Eunice is helping Stella with the baby while Stanley hosts another poker game. Stella tells Eunice that she cannot accept Blanche's story of the rape and go on living with Stanley; she has agreed to Blanche's being committed to a mental asylum. As the men play poker, Stella and Eunice collude with Blanche's fantasy that she is going to stay in the country. Blanche panics when a doctor and nurse arrive to take her away but eventually leaves calmly, escorted by the gentlemanly doctor. Stanley comforts the weeping Stella, but it seems he has good cause to believe that life will go on just as it did before Blanche came to New Orleans.

Scene summaries and commentaries

Target your learning

- How does Williams develop his themes, settings and characters as the dramatic action unfolds? (**AO1**)
- What dramatic methods does Williams use to shape the audience's responses at crucial points in the play? (**AO2**)

Scene I (pages 3–15)

▲ The action takes place in Stella and Stanley's cramped and untidy apartment – a marked contrast to Belle Reve, the now-lost ancestral mansion

It is early May in Elysian Fields, a shabby but vibrant working-class multicultural street in New Orleans' French Quarter (the Vieux Carré). Two young men, Stanley Kowalski and Harold Mitchell, known as 'Mitch', arrive at the apartment Stanley shares with his wife, Stella. Stanley has brought home a package of butcher's meat which he tosses to Stella before he and Mitch leave for the bowling alley. Stella soon goes after them to watch. At this point a stranger arrives, carrying a suitcase; it is Stella's elder sister, Blanche DuBois. Eunice, Stella's neighbour and landlady, lets Blanche into the Kowalskis' apartment with her key while a Negro Woman who had been chatting to Eunice offers to go and fetch Stella.

Once inside the apartment, it is clear Blanche thinks little of the cramped and untidy place and she is rather frosty with Eunice, who leaves her to herself. Blanche seems very highly strung and drinks a large whisky before carefully replacing the bottle and washing the glass. When Stella returns, the sisters seem pleased to see each other, but Stella is worried by Blanche's hyperactive and excitable state; Blanche admits her bad nerves have forced her to take a leave of absence from her job as a schoolteacher in Laurel, Mississippi.

Blanche makes some extremely insensitive remarks about Stella's home, her looks and her working-class Polish-American husband. Stella strongly defends Stanley and is obviously madly in love with him. Blanche also tells Stella they have lost Belle Reve, the family's ancestral mansion in the country, describing the long, drawn-out decline and deaths of all their relatives and blaming Stella for leaving her to face things alone. Stella is reduced to tears and goes into the bathroom to wash her face.

Stanley arrives back from bowling and he and Blanche assess each other warily. He offers her a whisky, surprised by how little is left in the bottle; she refuses, telling him she rarely drinks. She is offended when he strips off his sweat-stained shirt in front of her. When Stanley asks about her husband, Blanche tells him that 'the boy' died, before declaring that she feels sick.

Build critical skills

Closely analyse how Williams establishes the relationship of Stanley and Stella in the opening scene. How do you interpret the symbolism of him bringing home the raw meat from the butchers' shop?

Build critical skills

Consider Williams' opening description of Elysian Fields at the start of Scene 1. Note how he employs vivid sensory description, from the smell of bananas and coffee in the warehouses down by the river to the sound of the jazz music. What function does this narrative description have, given it is available only to readers of the script and not the theatre audience?

Context

New Orleans is divided into various districts, each with its own distinctive ambience; Elysian Fields is in the Vieux Carré or French Quarter, the most famous and atmospheric part of the city. During the late nineteenth and early twentieth centuries many immigrants settled here and the district developed a uniquely vibrant bohemian atmosphere, which makes it a major tourist attraction to this day.

Taking it further ▶

Read the first scene two or three times and watch a filmed performance if possible. Analyse how Williams arouses the reader's interest in this first scene.

◀ A New Orleans streetcar similar to the one that Blanche travels on

Context

Blanche relates the journey she has taken to reach Stella's home in 'Elysian Fields', riding a 'street-car named Desire' before transferring to another 'called Cemeteries'. In hindsight it seems clear that this journey is an allegorical representation of her tragic downfall, as in Greek mythology the Elysian Fields were a paradise for the dead.

> Top ten quotation

Commentary The essence of drama is conflict, and here Williams introduces both the tragic protagonist of his drama and her antagonist. In this scene the audience may be confused by Blanche; on the one hand her hysterical narcissism, social snobbery and crass insensitivity are off-putting, but on the other it is clear that she is physically, emotionally and psychologically very frail. The contrast with her brother-in-law, the 'gaudy seed-bearer' Stanley, who hurls a package of meat at Stella like a primitive hunter returning with his kill, could hardly be more extreme. There is an obvious level of sexual innuendo underlying his words and actions which is confirmed by the raucous amusement of the Negro Woman and Eunice, as well as Stella's excited response. Of Stella herself we learn relatively little, although it is clear both from the stage directions and her speech that she and Blanche are not of the same social class as the other characters who surround them. Although Blanche has come to stay with Stella and Stanley in Elysian Fields, she is dressed as if for a party in the Garden District, where the wealthy aristocrats of the Old South built their grand mansions and looked down on the racially mixed inhabitants of the Vieux Carré.

Context

Blanche's dress, manner and behaviour in this first scene places her firmly outside the context of the Vieux Carré. Williams makes use of the classic 'fish out of water' literary trope here, situating his central protagonist in a totally alien new situation. Comedy – or, as in *Streetcar*, tragedy – emerges as the character either learns to adapt to their new environment, or fails to. The motif goes back as far as Aesop's fable of *The Town Mouse and the Country Mouse* and is fundamental to Hans Christian Andersen's tragic fairy tale of *The Little Mermaid*.

Context

The 'blue piano' evokes the sound for which New Orleans has become world famous – so-called 'Dixieland' jazz and blues, a uniquely American blend of black African and European popular music which seems to embody the bohemian laid-back multicultural ambience of the city.

Commentary The audience hears two very different types of music in this scene which evoke both Blanche's new surroundings and her tragic past. Unlike the 'blue piano' music which is designed to suggest the atmosphere of New Orleans, the Varsouviana polka music is a non-naturalistic sound effect heard only in Blanche's imagination and by no other characters on stage. It symbolises her husband's suicide, the tragic event which wrecked her life; hearing it sends her into an extreme state of panic and fear which only ends when she hears the terrible sound of a gunshot.

Already haunted by her young husband's suicide, Blanche describes those hideous memories and dreams of the past which sent her half-mad during her final years at Belle Reve. Because dreams cross the boundaries of waking and sleeping they encapsulate a liminal (threshold) state very suitable for exploring the shadowy borderlands of the imagination. Blanche's dialogue is saturated with a series of Gothic horrors – grotesquely inflated corpses, burning bodies, the agonies of the dying and the sound of the death rattle – all presided over by the Angel of Death himself:

I, I, I took the blows in my face and my body! All of those deaths! The long parade to the graveyard! Father, mother! Margaret, that dreadful way! So big with it, it couldn't be put in a coffin! But had to be burned like rubbish! You just came home in time for the funerals, Stella. And funerals are pretty compared to deaths. Funerals are quiet, but deaths – not always. Sometimes their breathing is hoarse, and sometimes it rattles, and sometimes they even cry out to you, 'Don't let me go!' Even the old, sometimes, say 'Don't let me go.' As if you were able to stop them! But funerals are quiet, with pretty flowers. And, oh, what gorgeous boxes they pack them away in! Unless you were there at the bed when they cried out, 'Hold me!' you'd never suspect there was the struggle for breath and bleeding. You didn't dream, but I saw!

Saw! Saw! And now you sit there telling me with your eyes that I let the place go! How in hell do you think all that sickness and dying was paid for? Death is expensive, Miss Stella! And old Cousin Jessie's right after Margaret's, hers! Why, the Grim Reaper had put up his tent on our doorstep! ... Stella. Belle Reve was his headquarters! (page 12)

Blanche's extreme emotional outburst here can be seen to foreshadow her terrified reaction to the arrival in Scene 9 of the strange Mexican Woman selling mementos to commemorate lost loved ones in the shape of 'gaudy tin flowers' for the dead. Blanche is so hyper-aware of the significance and symbolism of death that we may deduce that as the last of the DuBois, hers may be the next name on the Grim Reaper's list.

Scene II (pages 15–24)

It is early evening on the day after Blanche's arrival in New Orleans. Blanche is taking a bath and Stella tells Stanley she is going to take Blanche out for the evening when he holds his poker night in the apartment. When Stella tells him that Belle Reve is lost, Stanley suspects Blanche has swindled Stella (and thus him) out of her share of the estate and searches Blanche's trunk looking for evidence despite Stella's horrified protests. Blanche emerges from the bathroom and flirts lightly with the sullen Stanley, but when she senses his suspicious mood she tries to protect Stella by asking her to fetch a cool drink from the local drugstore. Blanche defends herself against Stanley's accusations and shows him the legal documents which relate to the loss of Belle Reve but he grabs some other papers from her trunk and begins to read them. Extremely distressed, Blanche seizes them back; they are her dead husband's love letters. The legal documents prove that Belle Reve was lost when the DuBois family could no longer pay the mortgage and Blanche describes how her forebears drank, gambled and whored away everything until only the house itself and the family graveyard remained.

'There are thousands of papers, stretching back over hundreds of years, affecting Belle Reve as, piece by piece, our improvident grandfathers and father and uncles and brothers exchanged the land for their epic fornications - to put it plainly!'

> Top ten quotation

Despite Stella's wish to keep the news from Blanche for a little longer, Stanley tells her that Stella is pregnant. Stella returns, the poker players arrive and the two sisters head off for their evening out.

Commentary Blanche takes the first of her many long hot baths here, which – given that the cramped apartment has only one bathroom – seems very selfish behaviour from a long-term guest. The bathing symbolises Blanche's doomed attempt to erase her sordid past; compare her behaviour here with that of Shakespeare's Lady Macbeth, who compulsively washes imaginary bloodstains from her hands after Duncan's murder, to hide the 'evidence' of her crime.

Because the French noun *rêve*, meaning 'dream', is masculine, the premodifying adjective meaning 'beautiful' should be *beau* rather than *belle*. How far do you think this 'mistake' may suggest that there is, therefore, something slightly wrong with Blanche's 'beautiful dream' from the outset?

TASK

Think about different ways in which the confrontation between Blanche and Stanley might be directed, before watching the 1951 film version. Analyse which character you feel emerges as the more sympathetic in this interpretation and how you think the director, Elia Kazan, has tried to shape the audience's responses to each of them.

CRITICAL VIEW

Names and naming are highly significant within this text. 'Blanche DuBois' and 'Stanley Kowalski' may be contrasted through the soft consonants of the former and the hard vowels of the latter and instantly reveal that whereas one is a Southern aristocrat of French descent, the other is a working-class northerner of Polish descent. Think, too, about the significance of Stella DuBois becoming Stella Kowalski. Today many women do not take their husband's surname upon marriage, suggesting a wish to resist having their identity subsumed into that of another person and recognition that names are symbolic markers of one's personal and social identity. Yet most women bear surnames passed on by a man – their father.

Stanley's resentful and suspicious attitude towards Blanche becomes increasingly clear in this scene and the audience may well find her more sympathetic than she at first appeared, given the tragic history of Belle Reve's decline and her current vulnerable position. Stanley senses that Blanche has invaded his territory and may prove a potential rival for Stella's affections; while he knows that Stella would never look at another man, given their passionate sexual connection, the arrival of his wife's last living blood relative threatens to raise the ghost of that aristocratic past from which Stanley has fought to isolate her. Beyond Stanley and Blanche's personal feelings for Stella lies a greater divide, that between the romanticised values and traditions of the Old South and the thrusting energetic pursuit of money and success in the post-war era, and both acknowledge the class divide between them. In terms of dramatic structure, note how Williams has artfully sectioned this scene into two parallel dialogues between Stanley and each of the sisters so that the audience sees him baffled and angered by the superior knowledge and understanding of first Stella and then Blanche.

The Kowalskis' apartment is the arena in which a faded Southern belle and her working-class brother-in-law fight for physical space and emotional territory, and the large trunk in which she stores everything she owns in the world can be seen to symbolise the dark currents of sexual attraction and repulsion which eddy between them. Here, suspecting that Blanche has swindled Stella (and thus him) out of her share of the Belle Reve inheritance, Stanley rakes through Blanche's belongings looking for evidence. As he rummages through her faded finery, the horrified Stella tells him that while her sister's things may look expensive, really they're just cheap fakes. Blanche later defends herself against Stanley's accusations and shows him a bunch of legal documents which prove her innocence; the truth is that Belle Reve was lost because the sisters' degenerate ancestors had drunk and gambled away their inheritance. Williams' use of the trunk as a symbolic prop here is an early example of his masterly stagecraft. Just as Belle Reve symbolises Blanche's lost identity as a Southern belle, so her trunk full of tatty costumes functions as the objective correlative of both her tragic past and also her precarious current existence. As Stanley remarks sneeringly to Stella as he raids the battered dressing-up box in which Blanche stores the pathetic costumes and props she needs in order to perform her chosen roles: 'What is this sister of yours, a deep-sea diver who brings up sunken treasures? Or is she the champion safe-cracker of all time?' Williams' stage directions seethe with violence as Stanley 'pulls open' the trunk, 'jerks out' her dresses and 'hurls' her furs about before he 'kicks' it shut. Later he 'seizes' her perfume bottle and 'slams it down' before 'shov[ing]' the trunk 'roughly open' again; when he finds her pathetic cache of love letters and poems from her dead husband, Allan Grey, he 'snatches them up' and 'rips off the ribbon' which binds them. Blanche's dialogue here strongly suggests that she knows this violent action both contaminates her past and threatens her future: 'Now you've touched them I'll burn them! … I hurt [Allan] the way you that you would like to hurt me, but you can't!' Her accusation clearly foreshadows his later destruction of her social and sexual identity.

TASK

Compare and contrast the way in which Blanche describes the loss of Belle Reve to Stanley in this scene with her speech about the same event to Stella in Scene I. What do you think might be the possible effects upon an audience of this juxtapositioning of dialogues?

Scene III 'The Poker Night' (pages 24–34)

Blanche and Stella return after their girls' night out to find the poker night in full swing. When his best friend Mitch leaves the game to talk to Blanche, Stanley throws a drunken tantrum and hurls a radio out of the window. Stella is furious at his coarse and aggressive behaviour and he is violent towards her. The sisters escape upstairs to Eunice's, but Stella returns to Stanley when he pleads for her and they go to bed. Mitch finds a distressed Blanche outside and tries to comfort her.

▲ The poker night, as performed in the 2009 London production of *A Streetcar Named Desire*

Commentary This is one of only two scenes in the play in which nearly all the characters appear – the other is Scene XI – and the only one which has its own title, 'The Poker Night'. The introductory stage directions here are quintessential Williams, and merit very close examination; there is more on this aspect of Williams' stagecraft in the section on stage directions on pages 39–42 of this study guide. The poker game is a vivid and ominous metaphor for the game of life itself, as it involves bluffing, playing the hand you've been dealt, taking your chances when they come and riding any streak of luck that happens to come your way. Stanley is the leader of the pack and lord of all he surveys; his drunken, bullying violence creates a sense of increasing danger and menace as he controls the scene. When Stella calls Stanley an 'animal thing' and runs from his drunken and bestial rage in fear, his primal roar of 'STELL-LAHHHHHH!' into the night has her returning to her savage mate as *'they come together with low, animal moans'*. Stella's passionate loyalty to her husband bodes ill for Blanche. The passionate relationship between Stanley and Stella is paralleled by Mitch's attraction to Blanche's mysterious aura of gentility and there is some comedy here amid the violence as the ladylike French-speaking belle dances with the awkward, shambling average Joe. They make an odd couple, and even though both have loved and lost, it seems a bad omen that, whereas Mitch is simple, honest and serious, Blanche is complex, deceitful and flighty.

> **TASK**
>
> Watch this scene in two of the film versions listed in the 'Taking it further' section (p.105 of this guide). Discuss the differences and similarities between the two versions with the other students in your class. Which do you find the more powerful, and why?

> **TASK**
>
> During Scene III the jazz music begins to mirror the violent dramatic action on stage; dissonant *'brass and piano sounds'* are heard and a *'low-tone clarinet moans'*. In what ways do you think the music adds to the audience's understanding of the stormy emotions at work here?

Scene IV (pages 34–41)

Despite Blanche's passionate attempts to persuade Stella to leave Stanley after the poker night debacle, Stella insists that she loves him. Blanche suggests that she and Stella contact a millionaire named Shep Huntleigh who can help them escape. Unknown to the sisters, Stanley has returned to the apartment and has overheard Blanche's harsh and hostile comments about him.

Commentary When Stella mentions that Stanley has gone off to 'get the car greased' it indicates her acceptance of casual violence as part and parcel of their passionate relationship. Indeed, she adopts a tone of gently amused tolerance, mildly suggesting to the horrified Blanche that 'when men are drinking and playing poker anything can happen. It's always a powder-keg. He didn't know what he was doing … he was as good as a lamb when I came back and he's really very, very ashamed of himself'. While Stella does not try to justify Stanley's aggressive behaviour, it is clear to Blanche (and to the audience) that she is sexually excited by his macho persona; she recalls their wedding night, when he smashed all the light bulbs using her shoe, with delight, although Blanche is horrified by his brutality. It seems ironic that the aristocratic DuBois sisters – Southern belles born and bred – have both ridden the literal and metaphorical streetcar which 'bangs through the Quarter, up one old narrow street and down another'; while Blanche now bitterly regrets this, however, Stella is still joyfully revelling in the journey. Blanche's painful admission, 'It [the streetcar] brought me here', refers not only to her scandalous past in Laurel, but also reaches further back in time: Blanche and Stella are the last of a family infamous for their 'epic fornications'. Despite the fact that the audience has just witnessed Stanley at his very worst, Blanche's cynical plan to inveigle Shep Huntleigh into financing their getaway makes it less easy to believe that she wants to leave New Orleans solely for Stella's sake. Williams creates a level of intense dramatic irony in this scene: while the audience is aware of Stanley's sinister eavesdropping, the two women remain totally unaware of his presence. It is clear that Blanche's hysterical outburst will provoke him to strike back at his enemy, knowing that while he may have triumphed in this particular battle, he still has to win the war.

Scene V (pages 42–49)

In the apartment upstairs, Eunice and Steve are fighting about Steve's alleged infidelity. Blanche is terrified when Stanley hints that he knows the truth about her past. Eunice and Steve make up and go out for a drink at the Four Deuces with Stanley. Blanche tells Stella how much she dreads growing old alone and that she is thinking about a safe future with Mitch. After Stella follows Stanley, Steve and Eunice to the bar, Blanche kisses a young man who arrives to collect a newspaper subscription before Mitch (whom she calls her *Rosenkavalier*) arrives to take her out on a date.

Commentary This is a scene of inexorably building tension. When Stanley mentions the travelling salesman Shaw who knew Blanche from the Flamingo Hotel, she knows the act she has been putting on for Mitch's benefit is in danger of unravelling, while her sexual attraction to the unknown young man is so inappropriate that in this context even the coarse and brutal relationship of Steve and Eunice looks 'normal'. In flirting with the young man Blanche reveals how much of her essential nature she is struggling to repress in order to play the part of Mitch's 'prim and proper' prospective fiancée. Her behaviour clearly foreshadows the revelation of the real reason she was run out of Laurel, although here she just manages to control herself: 'Run along now! . . . I've got to be good and keep my hands off children'. Blanche, an 'epic fornicator' like all the rest of her family, hopes that marrying Mitch will help keep the lid on her wayward sexual desires.

TASK

Read the final stage directions in this scene and think about key aspects of Williams' stagecraft here (page 41). How and why does this tableau render dialogue unnecessary here in your opinion?

Build critical skills

Analyse how Williams presents Blanche's predatory sexual overtures to the Young Man in this scene. From a psychological critical perspective, how far can her behaviour here be traced back to the trauma and guilt she feels over the loss of her first love, Allan Grey?

Scene VI (pages 50–57)

Blanche and Mitch's date is not a great success; her nerves are in tatters at the thought of Stanley revealing the truth about her. At the end of the evening, however, they open up to each other and Blanche tells him about her young husband. Tortured by his homosexuality, Allan shot himself in the mouth after she found him with another man and revealed her disgust at his behaviour. Mitch comforts Blanche and tells her that they should be together: **'Could it be – you and me, Blanche?'**

Top ten quotation

Commentary Blanche's encounter with the Young Man in the previous scene is juxtaposed with the very different way she orchestrates her relationship with Mitch here. Blanche assumes the role of the doomed courtesan Marguerite, heroine of Alexandre Dumas' nineteenth-century tragic romance *La Dame aux Camélias*, casting the hapless Mitch as her much younger lover, Armand, before referring to his physical strength by calling him 'Samson', a reference to the Old Testament strongman betrayed by the fatal temptress Delilah. In scripting a scene in which she can play the role of the tragic Marguerite to Mitch's innocent young lover, Armand, she shows yet again her tendency to wilful self-dramatisation. The richness and complexity of Williams' dramaturgy is shown in his merging of aural and verbal symbolism; as the Varsouviana polka music plays in the background to externalise the memory of Allan's death, Blanche tells Mitch how falling in love had illuminated her world with a 'blinding light' which was brutally extinguished when he killed himself.

While Blanche is technically Mitch's social and intellectual superior, it shows how far she has fallen that she now needs him far more than he needs her. What Blanche chooses to reveal and conceal here is crucial. Telling Mitch the shocking truth about Allan's suicide in fact brings them closer, because Mitch has also loved and lost; indeed his sympathetic response may suggest that if Blanche had been equally frank about the aspects of her past she continues to withhold from him, he might just have forgiven these too. However, Blanche's failure to let in the light here foreshadows the end of their tentative relationship, because what she has decided must remain hidden, Stanley is sure to disclose.

Scene VII (pages 58–63)

It is a *'late afternoon in mid-September'* and Stella is preparing a birthday meal for Blanche. Stanley arrives home and while Blanche sings happily to herself in the bathroom, he reveals what he has discovered about her past. After the loss of Belle Reve, Blanche had moved into a low-rent hotel called the Flamingo, from which she was eventually evicted because of her promiscuous behaviour; she had been fired from her teaching post because an angry parent told the principal that Blanche was having an affair with his 17-year-old son. To Stella's horror, Stanley has told Mitch everything.

Commentary After the apparently hopeful ending of the previous scene, this one seems to begin positively as Stella prepares a birthday supper and Blanche warbles away in the bathroom. Yet the mood completely changes as Stanley arrives home in triumph with proof of Blanche's sexual misbehaviour; once more Williams creates intense dramatic contrast. Blanche's failure to be honest with Mitch at the end of the previous scene was undoubtedly cowardly and deceitful, yet the audience is surely aware that Stanley, when allocating the blame for her downfall, is motivated by more than simply an honest desire to protect Mitch. The fact that Stanley metaphorically stabs Blanche in the back by telling Stella the truth without giving her a chance to defend herself recalls Scene IV, when he deliberately concealed himself to eavesdrop on the sisters; on both occasions he reveals the kind of animal cunning that makes him such a dangerous enemy.

Williams creates a brilliantly uneasy mismatch here as moments of black comedy blur into a far more disturbing picture. Yet again – and with some justification – Stanley is driven crazy by Blanche's 'Washing out some things' and 'Soaking in a hot tub' in his bathroom; when she asks him to wait a little longer – 'Possess your soul in patience!' – he replies, 'It's not my soul I'm worried about', implying he needs to use the toilet. Yet lurking below this crude humour is a sinister metaphorical wish to soil the place in which Blanche seeks to purify herself. Once again music serves to heighten tension and create dramatic irony, by juxtaposing Blanche's singing with Stanley's remorseless demolition of her fantasy future with Mitch. Note that Williams' stage directions show that Blanche's singing and Stanley's revelation of the truth about her take place 'contrapuntally'; the term **contrapuntal** is used here to convey the unbridgeable gulf between the two enemies and the melodramatic – almost operatic – heightened tension of the scene. Stella's increasingly panic-stricken clichés – 'Lower your voice!'; 'What – contemptible – lies!'; 'It's pure invention!'; 'I don't want to hear any more!' – show that she is in deep denial. Ominously, Stanley reveals to Stella that the inhabitants of Laurel believed Blanche to be mad as well as bad; his contact Shaw heard she was regarded 'as not just different but downright loco – nuts'. Later, when he tells Stella that he has bought Blanche a ticket back to Laurel for the following Tuesday he declares, 'Her future is mapped out for her'. Thanks to him, this is wholly true.

contrapuntal: a description of polyphonic music in which the various parts are very clearly differentiated; in marked contrast to the original melody.

Scene VIII (pages 64–69)

'Three-quarters of an hour later' Blanche, Stella and Stanley are seated around the birthday table, but Mitch's chair is empty. It is clear that he has rejected Blanche following Stanley's revelation of the truth about her past. The tension builds until Stanley gives Blanche her birthday present – a bus ticket back to Laurel. Stella is appalled by Stanley's brutal malice and they argue fiercely about Blanche once more. The situation brings on Stella's labour and immediately Stanley takes her to hospital, leaving Blanche alone in the apartment.

▲ The tension at Blanche's birthday party builds…

Build critical skills

As Blanche's birthday falls on 15 September, her astrological sign is that of Virgo the Virgin, while Stanley, who was born 'just five minutes after Christmas', comes under the sign of Capricorn the Goat. Why do you think Williams chose these signs to symbolise them?

Commentary By now the conflict is ratcheting up towards the play's dramatic climax as Stanley determines to kick Blanche out of the apartment. For the first time she defends herself when he insults her. Stella, angrier than we have ever seen her before, tells Stanley that Blanche was innocent and trusting before 'people like you abused her', which surely implies that she expects Stanley to make her sister suffer too. Perhaps Stanley's animal magnetism has already changed Stella – or just liberated something similar which was already buried deep inside her. Williams uses the Kowalskis' dialogue to stress the growing gulf between them at this point; as Stella's speech becomes more formal and educated, Stanley's becomes more and more colloquial and fragmentary. Although the play predates it by about 25 years, in sociolinguistic terms the Kowalskis' dialogue in this scene can be seen as a fictional representation of Howard Giles' Communication Accommodation Theory (CAT). This theory examines how and why people alter their speech to stress or minimise their social differences. Giles argues that when speakers feel positive and cooperative their speech styles tend to converge to create rapport, whereas when they are at odds with each other they tend to diverge as they move to emphasise the social distance between them.

Context

The song 'Paper Moon' symbolises Blanche's relationship with Mitch. As she sings 'It's a Barnum and Bailey world/ Just as phony as it can be/But it wouldn't be make-believe/ If you believed in me' it seems clear her future happiness depends on Mitch's continuing to believe that the act she's been putting on for his benefit is real. You can listen to Nat King Cole perform the song on YouTube.

TASK

Think about alternative ways of performing this scene which might suggest different motivations for Stanley's actions and thus other ways of interpreting his character. Work with a group of students if possible.

Stella's disgusted attack on Stanley's table manners sends him into a fury because it so clearly demonstrates the radical difference between the sisters' upbringing and his own; using an image drawn from the game of poker he yells, 'What do you two think you are? A pair of queens?'.

It is during this scene that Stanley famously declares himself ready, willing and able to make a good life for himself in 'the land of the free and the home of the brave':

> I am not a Polack. People from Poland are Poles, not Polacks. But what I am is one hundred per cent American, born and raised in the greatest country on earth and proud as hell of it, so don't ever call me a Polack.

Top ten quotation

Stanley reminds Stella how he changed her from a genteel Southern belle initially repulsed by his crude passion into a willing sexual partner:

> When we first met, me and you, you thought I was common. How right you was, baby. I was common as dirt. You showed me the snapshot of the place with the columns. I pulled you down off them columns and how you loved it, having them coloured lights going! And wasn't we happy together, wasn't it all okay till she showed here?

Top ten quotation

These words indicate that it is a jealous fear of Blanche which makes him so determined to destroy her.

Stella's anger at Stanley's cruelty represents a potential rebellion which is cut short when she goes into labour. The timing of this event is a massive stroke of luck for him, as the baby symbolises their unbreakable connection and is Stella's main reason for finally siding with him against her sister. Over and above this, Stella's labour ensures that Blanche will be left alone and unprotected in the apartment. Note that the Varsouviana polka is used differently at the end of this scene; *'rising with sinister rapidity'*, it is no longer linked solely with the death of Allan Grey, but presages another defining crisis in Blanche's life. Ominously, at the beginning of the next scene, the Varsouviana becomes *'rapid'* and *'feverish'*.

Scene IX (pages 69–75)

'A while later that evening' Mitch arrives and challenges Blanche about what Stanley has told him. Blanche says that while the stories are true, she was seeking love and comfort after the death of her husband and wanted to escape the harsh world in which she found herself. Mitch rejects her as unfit to be his wife and live in the same house as his dying mother. He tries to force her to have sex but when she shouts 'Fire! Fire! Fire!' out of the window he leaves at once.

Commentary When Mitch turns on the light it is an aggressive act designed to unveil the 'real' Blanche hidden behind the old-fashioned Southern belle persona she has relied upon to charm him. On their previous date she lit a candle to make believe they were in Paris, the city of romance; now Mitch turns on a much harsher light which destroys her false veneer of respectability and prefigures his attempt to rape her. The appearance of the Mexican flower seller in this scene terrifies Blanche, who presumably interprets her cry of '*Flores para los muertos*' ('flowers for the dead') as an eerie premonition of her own fate.

This scene, which was apparently Williams' own favourite, brilliantly juxtaposes black comedy and lyrical tragedy. Blanche's vivid dialogue encompasses a scornful description of herself living at a hotel called the 'Tarantula Arms' like 'a big spider! That's where I brought my victims!' as well as a poignantly lyrical description of Mitch as 'a cleft in the rock of the world that I could hide in!'. Blanche had pinned all her hopes on marrying Mitch because she had felt it might prevent her hitching another ride on the fatal 'street-car named Desire', but his rejection signals the death of all her hopes for a peaceful and secure future. Blanche's lies are an escapist strategy designed to block out a reality she finds too harsh to bear, but with no one left to lie to, her only remaining audience is herself.

Context

The Día de Muertos (Day of the Dead) is celebrated throughout Mexico on 31 October each year. Families and friends come together to remember their lost loved ones and to take part in commemorative celebrations designed to support and comfort the dead on their final journey. Altars are built and decorated with brightly coloured and sometimes rather sinister objects of folk art, often skulls, skeletons and other souvenirs and memorabilia such as the Mexican Woman's tin flowers and crowns. Why do you think Williams has made use of this peasant tradition at this crucial point in the play?

Build critical skills

Analyse the way in which the Mexican Woman's cry of 'Flores para los muertos' near the end of Scene IX triggers Blanche's memories of the horrors she witnessed in the family's last years at Belle Reve and her efforts to compensate for that sickness and suffering by sleeping with the young soldiers from the local army camp.

TASK
Discuss with the other students in your class Williams' use of the Mexican Woman. Do you find the potent visual symbolism of the flower seller too melodramatic here, or can his use of this device be justified in terms of its powerful dramatic effect?

Scene X (pages 75–81)

Stanley returns from the hospital to find Blanche dressed for a society ball. Drunk and delusional, she informs him she will soon be leaving for a Caribbean cruise with her former beau, the Texas oil millionaire Shep Huntleigh. The sexual tension which has been building between them for months begins to spiral out of control as Stanley puts on the silk pyjamas he wore on his wedding night. As she tries to get past him Stanley blocks her way; the terrified Blanche smashes a bottle and threatens to slash his face with it. Stanley grabs her and carries her to the bed to rape her, declaring **'We've had this date with each other from the beginning!'**

Top ten quotation

TASK
As Blanche's make-believe world crumbles, so does Williams' set. Three New Orleans characters are visible to both Blanche and the audience: a prostitute, an alcoholic and a thief. How far do you feel that these characters can be seen as representations of Blanche herself? What is your response to Williams' use of visual symbolism here?

Commentary Drunk, confused and wearing a 'soiled and crumpled' party dress she would normally have been ashamed to be seen in, Blanche makes a horribly sad Cinderella figure here, shuffling about in her 'scuffed silver slippers' talking to the only audience she has left – herself. At first it seems Stanley has returned from the hospital in a reasonably friendly mood, but, as so often, they misunderstand each other, and the atmosphere quickly turns poisonous. Blanche tries to telephone for help, but the external world is once again presented as a dangerous jungle which can offer no support.

There is a tension between the immediate build-up to Stanley's assault on Blanche, which seems haphazard and unplanned, and its dramatic function as the inevitable climax of their deadly power struggle. Stanley's comment that they have 'had this date from the beginning' ties in with Williams' decision to have the rape take place off stage; there is no room for doubt as to whether this act has actually taken place, given that it has been so clearly foreshadowed by his invasion of Blanche's private possessions – including her love-letters from Allan – at the beginning of the play. Moreover, since sexual domination has always been Stanley's modus operandi when it comes to dealing with Stella, the utterly taboo act of raping her sister has a hideous internal logic. The sexual desire he has discovered and stoked within Stella is twisted into a nightmarish kind of 'incest by proxy' as he costumes himself once again in the silk pyjamas he bought for his wedding night.

There is an uncomfortable grain of truth in Stanley's declaration that he and Blanche had had their 'date' from the beginning; the seething tension between them might have been expressed most often in social, economic and cultural terms, but there was always something deeply sexual about his prurient interest in her promiscuous past and her coyly flirtatious response to his macho posturing. Before attacking her physically, Stanley first rapes her emotionally and psychologically by demolishing her pathetic Shep Huntleigh fantasy, as if to underline the fact that sex with him is her only option. In this context, Stanley's brutality seems so extreme and all-encompassing that the rape can be seen to represent the annihilation of the Old South by the thrusting post-war world.

Build critical skills

Analyse how far Stanley and Blanche appear to wilfully misunderstand each other in this crucial scene. When he arrives home from the hospital he seems to be in a rather good-tempered mood, but the scene ends in a horrific rape. Trace the aspects of Blanche's behaviour that always appear to antagonise Stanley (such as her drinking and fantasising) and try to work out why he explodes into violence on this particular occasion.

A much less cynical and nihilistic take on the inevitable destruction of Blanche's world is encapsulated in the florid epigraph to the 1939 film of Margaret Mitchell's romantic saga *Gone With The Wind* (1936). As the credits roll, iconic images evoking the spirit of the Old South provide the backdrop, including peaceful fields being farmed by contented slaves, the majestic Mississippi river and a gaudy scarlet sunset. You can watch the opening credits of the film on YouTube (the web address can be found on page 106).

Immediately after the title credits roll, the film begins with this nostalgic elegy:

There was a land of Cavaliers and Cotton Fields called the Old South. Here in this pretty world, Gallantry took its last bow. Here was the last ever to be seen of Knights and their Ladies Fair, of Master and of Slave. Look for it only in books, for it is no more than a dream remembered; a Civilization gone with the wind …

Scene XI (pages 81–90)

'Some weeks later' Stella and Eunice are packing Blanche's trunk while she finishes bathing and the men play poker. They are awaiting the arrival of a doctor and nurse to take Blanche to an insane asylum, but Blanche, who has clearly crossed the border into outright madness by now, thinks she is going to the country to visit Shep Huntleigh. Stella tells Eunice she cannot allow herself to believe Blanche's assertion that Stanley raped her, and Eunice reassures her that she has no other choice: **'Life has got to go on'**. When the doctor and nurse arrive, Blanche panics. Stanley and his friends subdue Blanche as Eunice holds Stella back; Mitch begins to cry and accuses Stanley of having reduced Blanche to this state, while the other men also mutter uncomfortably. Finally, the gentlemanly doctor earns Blanche's trust (**'I have always depended on the kindness of strangers',**) and she leaves quietly. Stella sobs bitterly, hugging the baby as Stanley tries to comfort her. The play ends as Steve announces, **'This game is seven-card stud'**. Life in Elysian Fields, it seems, will go on as if Blanche DuBois had never been there at all.

Commentary After the previous climactic rape scene, Scene XI is a kind of **coda**. In many ways this sombre and downbeat scene – in which all the main characters appear for only the second time – functions as a grotesque inversion of the poker night, in which the electrifying excitement of the drunken, violent Stanley being wrangled into the shower by his buddies is horrifyingly re-enacted as the pitiful, terrified Blanche is wrestled to the floor before being taken off to the asylum.

Blanche does not wish to pass Stanley and his poker buddies on her way through the apartment as they are by now irrelevant to her; the last of her trademark long hot baths suggests she now wishes ritually to wash away the 'stain' of her rape in order to be 'pure' for her imaginary beau, Shep Huntleigh. Blanche's desire to appear innocent and virginal is symbolised by her choice of costume for her departure; although Eunice compliments the 'pretty blue jacket', which Stella thinks is 'lilac coloured', Blanche declares: 'You're both mistaken. It's Della Robbia blue. The blue of the robe in the old Madonna pictures'.

Given that Stanley mocked Blanche as 'the Queen of the Nile' earlier in the play, it is interesting that Shakespeare's indelible image of Cleopatra preparing for death, attended by her two faithful handmaidens, is evoked here. Unlike Charmian and Iras, however, who both choose to die along with their mistress, the loyalty of Stella and Eunice is fatally compromised. While it seems that Blanche has finally given up trying to reinvent reality and has blocked it out once and for all, she is not the only woman in an extreme state of denial here. Stella might as well sing her baby to sleep with 'Paper Moon', as she has willingly decided to live in a fantasy world; denying Blanche's story and believing in her 'madness' allows Stella to avoid the truth about her husband. While their gentle kindness towards Blanche suggests that at some deep level they both know the

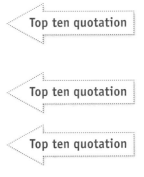

Top ten quotation

Top ten quotation

Top ten quotation

coda: a dramatic postscript or afterthought.

Context

For further information on the American South and on Tennessee Williams as a Southern writer, see the *Themes* and *Contexts* sections of this guide.

Top ten quotation

truth, Stella and Eunice also know that that truth must remain unspoken so life can go on. Steve's comment **'This game is seven-card stud'** highlights the idea that while men seem to hold all the cards, women are forced to collude with them and pretend to believe their hollow bluffing.

Like Blanche, who is wearing 'Della Robbia blue', Stella's baby son is wrapped in a pale blue blanket which makes the triptych of mother, father and child at the end of the play a warped visual image of the Holy Family. Yet in this Darwinist 'survival of the fittest' society in which Blanche must be sacrificed to ensure Stanley's future, Williams questions whether everything is really as secure as it may seem. While Stella and Eunice know deep down that the baby represents the future and that therefore his need for security must take precedence, should we not fear, given that Stanley's behaviour is often extremely childlike, that one day Stanley will become just as jealous of his son's ties to Stella as he was of Blanche's?

Taking it further ▶

In Charlotte Brontë's *Jane Eyre*, written 100 years before *A Streetcar Named Desire*, another wife (Jane) asserts the madness of her husband's sexual partner (i.e. his dead wife) to justify his oppressive actions towards her 'rival' and legitimise her own continuing relationship with the father of her child. You might compare these two texts through the lens of feminist criticism and look at the extent to which the ways in which they deal with this similar theme reflects their radically different contemporary cultural milieux.

Themes

Target your learning

- What are the key themes of *A Streetcar Named Desire* and how does Williams develop them as the dramatic action unfolds? (**AO1**)
- What dramatic methods does Williams use to illustrate his key themes? (**AO2**)

The Italian author Primo Levi declared in his book *Other People's Trades* (1989) that 'all authors have had the opportunity of being astonished by the beautiful and awful things that the critics have found in their works and that they did not know they had put there'. Often, we have no means of knowing an author's intentions; what is important is the impact of the text on a reader or, in the case of a play, an audience. Even if an author has written explicitly about what he or she sees as the key thematic content of a work, that does not preclude other themes from coming to the attention of particular readers. Moreover, Williams' work cannot be divorced from the circumstances of his life, values, assumptions, gender, race and class, and just as he was a product of his age, so you are a product of yours. How you respond to *A Streetcar Named Desire* will depend on your own experiences, ideas and values and it is well worth thinking about how readers and audiences decide what the major themes of any literary text are.

Reality and illusion

Williams' famously poetic stage directions, in which Blanche is likened to a fluttering white moth who must avoid the light, suggest that she craves 'magic' because the truth about post-war America is too harsh to bear. Her antagonist, Stanley, on the other hand, is imbued with an earthy – even brutal – sense of realism which makes him loathe her 'Barnum and Bailey world' and do all he can to trash it. Thus the theme of fantasy and reality plays out on stage as another aspect of the desperate struggle between the play's protagonist and antagonist. Which character you decide to side with is up to you. When Stanley rapes Blanche he uses the disturbingly incongruous word 'date' to describe what he has planned for her, as if they are lovers who have passed a pleasant evening in each other's company; thus he ensures that her Shep Huntleigh illusion is utterly destroyed. The question of how far illusions are helpful or necessary remains; ironically, as Felicia Hardison Londré notes, it is only when Blanche actually tells Mitch the truth for once – about the death of Allan Grey – that she finally gains 'what she has not been able to achieve in two months or so of artful deceit: a proposal of marriage' (Londré in M. Roudané, *The Cambridge Companion to Tennessee Williams*, 1997).

According to Christopher Innes, *Streetcar* contains all of Williams' 'major themes: the ambiguous nature of sexuality, the betrayal of faith, the corruption of modern America, the over-arching battle of artistic sensitivity against physical materialism' (Innes in S. McEvoy).

Liebestod: (from the German meaning 'love death') an erotic union achieved by lovers only through or after death.

Taking it further ▶▶

In both F. Scott Fitzgerald's *The Great Gatsby* (1925) and John Steinbeck's *Of Mice and Men* (1936) the tragic central characters' dreams are ended with a violent gunshot. Look at these two novels and think about how far you agree that they — and *Streetcar* — present dreams as transient and illusory, but rare and valuable nonetheless.

Death and desire

Streetcar was one of the first post-war dramas to present a range of characters for whom sex was of huge importance as a factor influencing their lives and relationships. One of the text's defining images — that of the streetcar — explicitly links sex and death, making it possible to see the play within the context of the *Liebestod* tradition.

At first glance it might seem a struggle to position *Streetcar* within this literary framework (after all, nobody dies at the end) but in fact the *Liebestod* theme may be seen to enhance (or parody) the romantic and tragic grandeur of Blanche's downfall, depending on your point of view.

Very early in the play the English teacher Blanche makes the first of her evocative and suggestive literary references when she likens the chain of events which culminated in the loss of Belle Reve to something 'Only Poe! Only Mr. Edgar Allan Poe!' could conceive, as her DuBois forebears went to rack and ruin through indulging in their 'epic fornications'. The specific situation to which she refers here — the fall of a once great family and their home — calls to mind Poe's Gothic horror story *The Fall of the House of Usher* (1839), with Blanche as the persecuted Madeline who is entombed, while still alive, by her twin brother. Blanche's awareness of her own fate is signalled by her horrified reaction to the Mexican Woman with her flowers for the dead, and while Stanley is her brother-in-law and not her brother, his rape does indeed consign her to a kind of death-in-life which seems to resemble Madeline's as she is 'entombed' within the walls of a lunatic asylum.

Like her husband Allan, whose homosexuality led directly to his death, Blanche is a figure for whom sex and death are fatally entwined. Following Allan's suicide, Blanche is left with a morbid fear of ageing, and in some ways her attraction to very young men suggests that in seducing them she hopes to recapture something of her own lost youth and innocence. Yet the love (or sex, or desire) with which Blanche tries to fight off death is also the direct cause of her tragic fall, the sickness as well as the cure.

Context

Blanche likens her experiences at Belle Reve to the Gothic horror stories of Edgar Allan Poe (1809-49). Poe, who died in poverty at the age of 40, was a master of the short story. *The Fall of the House of Usher* is a characteristic work that you might enjoy reading; another is *The Masque of the Red Death*.

Context

Two of the most famous texts from within the English literary tradition to deal with the *Liebestod* theme are Shakespeare's *Romeo and Juliet* (c. 1595) and Emily Brontë's *Wuthering Heights* (1847), while in Stephenie Meyer's popular teenage *Twilight* series, the heroine, Bella Swan, can only achieve a permanent relationship with Edward Cullen after she too has become a vampire.

On several further occasions throughout the play, literary references are used to evoke images of famous women, real and fictional, who have suffered and died for love. Introducing herself to Mitch during Stanley's poker night, Blanche tells him that she's an English teacher struggling to 'instil a bunch of bobby-soxers and drug-store Romeos with reverence for Hawthorne and Whitman and Poe!'. The reference to 'Romeos' is doubly ironic, in view of her fatal attraction to underage boys, while the mention of Nathaniel Hawthorne evokes the image of Hester Prynne, the heroine of his most famous novel *The Scarlet Letter* (1850), who is shunned and scorned by her narrow-minded Puritan community for adultery and fornication.

Later Blanche assumes the role of the doomed courtesan Marguerite, heroine of Dumas' tragic romance *La Dame aux Camélias*, casting the hapless Mitch as her much younger lover, Armand, before referring to his physical strength by calling him 'Samson', a reference to the Old Testament strongman betrayed by the fatal temptress Delilah. Finally, and perhaps most ominously, however, it is Stanley who provides the last literary figure with whom we are invited to compare *Streetcar*'s doomed heroine. He viciously parodies Blanche's 'hoity-toity' affectations by likening her to Cleopatra: '. . . lo and behold the place has turned into Egypt and you are the Queen of the Nile!'.

Marginality and madness: the outcast

According to Alycia Smith-Howard and Greta Heintzelman, Williams 'is celebrated as "a poet of the human heart" and as the "Laureate of the Outcast"' (Smith-Howard and Heintzelman, *Critical Companion to Tennessee Williams*, 2005). In 1939, the playwright told his literary agent Audrey Wood, 'I have only one major theme for my work, which is the destructive power of society on the sensitive non-conformist individual' and in *Streetcar* Blanche is indeed cast out of society because she refuses to conform to conventional moral values. Forced to confess her sins, she is then viciously punished.

The ancient Greek word for tragedy means 'goat-song' and Blanche is surely the scapegoat here, cast out of society in order to bear the sins of others. While Stanley, previously dismissed as an uncouth '**Polack**', is socially on the up, Blanche is gradually stripped of her psychological, sexual, financial and cultural

Top ten quotation

identity. At the end of the play, Blanche is forced to retreat into a state of denial, her mental health all but shattered, in order to shield her fragile sense of self from Stanley's brutal truth.

Context

The American novelist Nathaniel Hawthorne (1804-64) often explored the darker side of human existence in his morally and psychologically intricate works, the most famous of which is *The Scarlet Letter*.

Characters

Target your learning

- How does Williams develop his characters as the dramatic action unfolds? (**AO1**)
- What dramatic methods does Williams use to shape the audience's responses to the characters? (**AO2**)

One of the most common errors made by students is to write about characters in literature as if they were real people as opposed to fictional constructs created to fulfil a range of purposes in different texts. When it comes to a play, the 'language' belonging to each character is a blueprint for their interpretation by different actors, and one important aspect of analysis is to consider the range of potential performances of a text.

Characters in a play are defined through language and action. What they do, what they say, how they say it, and what other characters say about them, determine the response of the audience. On stage these techniques of characterisation are enhanced by costume, gesture, facial expression, proxemics (the distance between actors which indicates the relationship between the characters) and other performance features.

As well as the brief sketches below, there is more information about the main characters in several other sections of this book, particularly the *Scene summaries and commentaries*, *Themes* and *Contexts*.

▲ Stella and Blanche in the 2014 London production of *A Streetcar Named Desire*

> **TASK**
>
> Look online at the painting 'Poker Night' (from *A Streetcar Named Desire*) (1948) by Thomas Hart Benton (1889–1975). Jessica Tandy, who created the role of Blanche, felt that this overtly sexualised image was a misrepresentation. How far do you agree with her view?

Main characters

Blanche DuBois

For many Williams fans, Blanche DuBois is his quintessential heroine, psychologically damaged, emotionally fragile, socially liminal and culturally dispossessed. When Eunice first sees her dressed in those utterly incongruous floating white clothes she asks: 'What's the matter, honey? Are you lost?'. Indeed she is; in fact Blanche is the archetypal lost soul, but Williams makes her an insensitive, prickly and often irritating character rather than one the audience necessarily identifies with and pities from the outset. Blanche is an ageing Southern belle on the wrong side of thirty, whose tragic and stormy life has led her to avoid reality in favour of what she dreamily refers to as 'magic'. As the play progresses, Blanche's instability grows as Stanley strips away her fantasy life and wrecks her relationship with Mitch. Haunted by all she has lost – her first love, her home, her culture, her dignity and her place in the world – her life is already a sexual, emotional and economic disaster zone when she arrives in Elysian Fields. Underneath her unpleasantly snobbish arrogance lies a vulnerable and damaged psyche. Loneliness and a lack of self-esteem has led her to come close to prostitution and she sees marrying Mitch as her only way out. However, Stanley's merciless persecution of her culminates in a brutal rape which triggers her complete mental breakdown.

Stanley Kowalski

Proud to be a second-generation Polish American, at the beginning of the play Stanley Kowalski appears to be a loyal friend, a passionate husband and a genial host. A decorated soldier who fought in World War II, Stanley is down-to-earth, forceful and practical; Blanche's genteel fictions and fantasies drive him crazy. At first he may well have the audience's sympathy when Blanche ignorantly refers to him as a 'Polack', and it is not hard to see that his hatred of her stems from the genteel Southern past she represents as well as her infuriating airs and graces. As time goes on, however, Stanley's behaviour towards Blanche becomes increasingly hostile and vicious to the point where it is clearly unjustified by any of her actions. By the time the play ends the audience has witnessed Stanley bullying his friends, abusing his pregnant wife and raping his fragile sister-in-law. The nature of Stanley's relationship with Stella is at the very heart of the play; the ways in which it alters, changes and deteriorates are profoundly influenced by Blanche's arrival in New Orleans. The final tableau of Stanley soothing the sobbing Stella may be seen to pose uncomfortable questions about the criteria by which Blanche has been socially excluded.

Stella Kowalski

Stella's name embodies the tension between her former life at Belle Reve and her new life in Elysian Fields; Blanche's 'Stella for star' has become Stanley's 'STELLLAHHHH!' Unlike her sister, Stella got away from Belle Reve during the war and made her way to New Orleans where she met Stanley; only during a time of such immense social, cultural and historical upheaval would the aristocratic Stella DuBois have met the working-class Stanley Kowalski. Like her sister, Stella is a sexually passionate woman and although she pities Blanche and wants to protect her, she refuses to allow herself to believe her accusation of rape. Stella's decision to go for fantasy over reality in the end seems to indicate that she is a DuBois born and bred after all.

Harold 'Mitch' Mitchell

Though on the surface Mitch seems lumbering, gauche and ungainly, he is a sensitive and kindly soul at heart. Teased as a 'mama's boy', Mitch wants to marry so that his mother can die in peace, knowing that he won't be left alone after her death. Mitch and Blanche, having both loved and lost, believe they can comfort one another. When Stanley tells him the truth about Blanche's past, however, Mitch feels Blanche has made a fool of him with her virginal Southern belle act and tries to force her to sleep with him; he weeps when she is taken away to the asylum. While some readers and audiences may see Mitch as a clownish character, others may view him as a tragic figure in his own right.

Eunice Hubbel

Stella's friend, neighbour and landlady, Eunice may foreshadow the life Stella will come to lead a few years down the line as she fights with her husband, the philandering Steve, before noisily making up with him. At the end of the play, although she assures Stella that she is right to reject Blanche's story of rape and has no choice but to stick with Stanley, Eunice nevertheless behaves with sensitivity towards Blanche.

Steve Hubbel

Eunice's husband Steve is one of Stanley's poker buddies. A loutish and lecherous drunk, he may well suggest what Stanley will become in the future. Interestingly, however, when Steve seems uneasy at Blanche's removal to the asylum, it suggests – albeit temporarily – that even Stanley's poker buddies are aware that they are witnessing something terrible. Steve has the very last line of the play, when in the absence of Stanley, who is outside the apartment comforting Stella, he announces that normal service in Elysian Fields has been resumed after Blanche's removal: **'This game is seven-card stud'**.

Taking it further ▶

Williams' presentation of sexual tension and class conflict as inextricably linked in the downfall of an iconic female protagonist echoes both Henrik Ibsen's *Hedda Gabler* (1890) and August Strindberg's *Miss Julie* (1888). Look at one or both of these plays. What similarities and differences in plot and character can you trace?

TASK

Depending on how Stella is played, her character could come across as more or less sympathetic. How would you choose to present her if you were directing the play, and what elements of Williams' characterisation and dialogue would sway your decision?

Top ten quotation

Build critical skills

Collate all the textual information that relates to Allan Grey and assess what Williams' representation of this gentle young man suggests about Blanche's past. How does he differ from the main flesh-and-blood male characters, Stanley and Mitch?

Other characters

Pablo

Another poker player, whose ethnic roots show the cultural diversity of Elysian Fields. He, too, is troubled by Blanche's removal.

Allan Grey

Although Allan Grey never appears on stage he is an extremely important character; Blanche has never got over her guilt at his death nor found another love to replace him. Blanche was an innocent 16-year-old when they married and, given the contemporary stigma around homosexuality, would have had no idea why her sensitive and artistic young husband was unable to consummate their marriage on the wedding night. The doomed Allan – whose extreme youth is encapsulated in the description of him as 'The Grey boy' – is a lost soul sacrificed on the altar of social bigotry. When Blanche discovers Allan with another man, it utterly destroys her happiness. All three of them then take off for the Moon Lake Casino on a manic drinking spree in a tragic attempt to pretend 'that nothing had been discovered'. Eventually, unable to stop herself, Blanche blurts out to Allan her feelings about his homosexuality; 'on the dance-floor – unable to stop myself – I'd suddenly said – "I know! I know! You disgust me …"'. Knowing that the secret he has tried so hard to conceal has been finally exposed, Allan runs outside and shoots himself by the lake. Blanche's memory of this event is so stark that she can recall the precise words spoken by the horrified onlookers who gathered by the body when she tells the story to Mitch in Scene VI.

Shep Huntleigh

Shep is another character present only in Blanche's memory. A former beau of hers, he comes to represent her last hope of escaping her past. Apparently an oil millionaire from Dallas, Texas, Blanche claims to have worn his 'ATO pin' when they were courting, which was a sign of 'going steady'. The character's name is also interesting. At the end of the play Blanche confuses the doctor who has come to take her to the asylum with her former beau. This seems highly significant given that the doctor can be seen as both a good 'shepherd' who guides and supports her and as a sinister 'hunter' who captures and entraps her.

Context

Shep's 'ATO pin' shows his affiliation to the Alpha Tau Omega college fraternity, founded in Virginia at the end of the Civil War in 1865. The brotherhood's aim was to unify the divided North and South in the aftermath of the conflict that had split the nation. Shep's membership of this elite aristocratic society is an index of his status as an old-school Southern gentleman and positions him as Stanley's social and cultural opposite number.

A Young Man

The Young Man comes to the Kowalskis' apartment when Blanche is waiting at home for Mitch to collect her for their date. Blanche is attracted to him and kisses him. On the one hand, he is an uneasy reminder of that obsession with very young men which resulted in Blanche being fired from her teaching post; on the other, he evokes the ghost of her tragic husband Allan Grey.

A Negro Woman

Another character who reveals the multicultural nature of the Vieux Carré, the Negro Woman appears in the first scene of the play, chatting to Eunice. She is amused by Stanley's unmistakable sexual posturing and when Blanche arrives she offers to fetch Stella from the bowling alley. In Scene X, just before Stanley rapes Blanche, she is seen outside the Kowalskis' apartment, rifling through a prostitute's stolen handbag.

A Mexican Woman

The blind Mexican Woman, who sells traditional funeral decorations, alarms Blanche with her eerie cry of '*Flores para los muertos*' – 'flowers for the dead'. She functions as a kind of **choric** figure, further heightening the play's links with classical tragedy.

choric resembling a chorus in drama or recitation.

Context

In classical Greek tragedy the chorus often represented ordinary people as opposed to the great heroes and gods who dominated the action on stage, expressing for the benefit of the audience those ideas and emotions the main characters were unable to voice, such as hidden fears or desires. It is possible to see both the Mexican Woman and the unseen but audible Tamale Vendor as fulfilling aspects of these functions in *Streetcar*.

A doctor and a nurse

When he arrives to take Blanche to the asylum the doctor refuses to have Blanche put into a straitjacket and leads her out of the Kowalskis' apartment by the arm in a rather courtly and gentlemanlike manner. In a final moment of immense pathos, it seems clear that Blanche has confused the doctor with her former beau, Shep Huntleigh. The nurse's harsh manner serves to highlight his much more sympathetic attitude.

Writer's methods: form, structure and language

Target your learning

- How does Williams develop his themes, settings and characters as the dramatic action unfolds? (**AO1**)
- What dramatic methods does Williams use to shape the audience's responses at crucial points in the play? (**AO2**)

This section is designed to offer you information about the form, structure and language of *A Streetcar Named Desire* in order to help you approach AO2, the Assessment Objective which requires you to analyse ways in which meanings are shaped in literary texts. In the next few pages each aspect of Williams' craft is covered separately in order to clarify the differences between them, but it is important to remember that these different strands frequently overlap and interact. Therefore this section begins with a discussion of the playwright's signature personal theory of 'plastic theatre' as a way of unifying any discussion of form, structure and language.

Putting it all together: 'plastic theatre'

In his production notes for his first major stage success *The Glass Menagerie* (1944), Williams discussed the need to create an overarching, holistic, organic theatrical experience to challenge what he saw as the limitations of conventional, realist theatre. For Williams, drama had to do more than merely reproduce 'reality'; he wanted to explore the ways in which theatrical performances could tap into a wider definition of the 'truth'. In a sense, knowing that his plays were about unconventional characters and themes, Williams rightly saw that they needed equally unconventional stage effects; his 'new, plastic theatre', he hoped, would then 'take the place of the exhausted theatre of realistic conventions':

> *Expressionism and all other unconventional techniques in drama have only one valid aim, and that is a closer approach to truth. When a play employs unconventional techniques, it is not, or certainly shouldn't be, trying to escape its responsibility of dealing with reality, or interpreting experience, but is actually or should be attempting to find a closer approach, a more penetrating and vivid expression of things as they are. The straight realistic play with its genuine Frigidaire and authentic ice-cubes, its characters who speak exactly as its audience speaks, corresponds to the academic landscape and has the same virtue of a photographic likeness. Everyone should know nowadays the unimportance of the photographic in art: that truth, life, or reality is an organic thing which the poetic imagination can represent or suggest, in essence, only through transformation, through changing into other forms than those which were merely present in appearance.*
>
> Tennessee Williams, *The Glass Menagerie*, 1944

For Williams, a play had to do more than merely reflect life as it was; it should try to express some universal insight into the human condition. His modes of dramatic expression are thus many, varied and complex and his concept of 'plastic theatre' places as much value on non-literary and non-verbal elements of drama, such as sound, lighting, movement, setting and design, as it does on dialogue in terms of their ability to convey theme and character. Thus the following section will draw attention to many of the non-naturalistic aspects of his work, such as his metaphorical scene descriptions, symbolic use of setting, props, music, sound and lighting, and patterned and poetic dialogue, because Williams saw all these elements as forming part of an organic and overarching dramatic experience. In fact, given his commitment to what might be seen as a kind of total or extreme theatre, worrying about whether to categorise, say, 'imagery' under the heading of form, structure or language completely misses the point. It is far better to think in terms of Williams' own notion of 'plastic theatre', and celebrate the fact that he hit upon a vivid, ambitious and pretty much all-encompassing view of the possibilities of the dramatic medium.

Many aspects of Williams' dramatic method are explored in other sections of this book, particularly the *Scene summaries and commentaries* on pages 3–20 of this guide.

Build critical skills

Expressionism is characterised by a replacement of objectivity and realism with a more subjective picture of the world. To express heightened states of emotion or intense personal experiences, ideas and emotions are presented in deliberately warped, artificial and/or unnatural ways. Expressionist drama often portrays the ongoing suffering and epiphanies of the protagonist episodically and sometimes uses bizarrely stylised or heightened speech styles. Locate and analyse examples of the expressionist features within *A Streetcar Named Desire*.

Form

The essence of a theatrical performance lies in its ephemeral nature, whereas the written text from which it springs is fixed and permanent. When you write about the form, structure and language of a play you must show a keen awareness of the ways in which the dramatic genre works and the specifically theatrical methods used by playwrights to present their ideas. If you remember that the printed version of *Streetcar* is above all a blueprint for performance, and that the play was written to be seen and heard in the company of others rather than read alone, you are on the right track. Unlike a novel or a poem, a play is not complete in its purely written form; it has to make the transition from page to stage. A theatre audience shares the same physical space as the actors performing; we are separate from the onstage action but eyewitnesses to it in real time and real space. Thus when we read rather than watch *Streetcar,* we are receiving the text in an incomplete, yet extremely rich and rewarding form.

If you look at a play written by Shakespeare or one of his contemporaries you will notice a striking lack of detailed stage directions, probably because the playwright himself was available to have some input into the staging of his own work. In the centuries since then, other playwrights have used brief stage directions to tell the actors how to behave, to whom they should direct their speech, or what tone of voice to adopt, but in many twentieth-century plays, including those of Williams, the stage directions go way beyond such practical and functional details. Indeed, Williams' precise, rich and often lyrical stage directions are often so thought-provoking that they offer an additional level of enjoyment to the reader which is unavailable to a theatre audience. One of the most characteristic elements of Williams' dramaturgy is the fact that while his characters are presented extremely realistically, his staging is often startlingly non-naturalistic. Part of *Streetcar's* power stems from watching his penetratingly observed and psychologically convincing characters use heightened and heavily patterned dialogue rich with linguistic motifs as they interact within a consciously stylised onstage world teeming with unusual and symbolic visual and sound effects.

In terms of genre or form, one of the most interesting aspects of *A Streetcar Named Desire* is the various ways in which we might choose to categorise it as, for instance, a twentieth-century American tragedy, a melodrama, or what Williams himself described as a 'memory play'. Generic categories, however, are not fixed but in a constant state of flux. As an active reader, you should aim to locate a range of interesting questions that lurk in the gaps between the apparently overlapping and occasionally contradictory dramatic sub-genres mentioned in this section. One of the most exciting aspects of *Streetcar* is the way in which it seems simultaneously polemical, political, poetic and romantic. In the end, perhaps Williams' artful blurring of literary genres allows us to see how a great writer can be startlingly innovative and original while still conforming to many traditional theatrical practices and conventions.

Twentieth-century American tragedy

Tragedy is the art form created to confront the most difficult experiences we face: death, loss, injustice, thwarted passion, despair.

Wallace in McEvoy, 2009

According to the Greek philosopher Aristotle, writing around 330BC, 'the structure of the best tragedy should be not simple but complex and one that represents incidents arousing fear and pity – for that is peculiar to this form of art'. In essence, a tragedy involves the downfall of a great man (the tragic hero) as the result of a reversal of fortune (*peripeteia*) which is the inevitable result of his own actions and involves the concept of *hamartia*, which is usually taken to mean a fatal character flaw. At the play's denouement, the tragic hero gains some insight (*anagnorisis*) into the nature of the human condition, fate or destiny and the will of the gods, while the onlookers are moved to feel pity and terror at what they have seen, thereby achieving a kind of spiritual cleansing in the process (*catharsis*). From the very beginning, it seems, the audience has always been as much a part of the tragic experience as the actors.

In his *Memoirs*, published about 30 years after he had written *Streetcar*, Williams declared:

> *I realise how very old-fashioned I am as a dramatist to be so concerned with classic form but this does not embarrass me, since I feel that the absence of form is nearly always, if not always, as dissatisfying to an audience as it is to me. I persist in considering Cat [on a Hot Tin Roof] my best work of the long plays because of its classical unities of time and place and the kingly magnitude of Big Daddy. Yet I seem to contradict myself. I write so often of people with no magnitude, at least on the surface. I write of 'little people'. But are there 'little people'? I sometimes think there are only little conceptions of people. Whatever is living and feeling with intensity is not little and, examined in depth, it would seem to me that most 'little people' are living with that intensity that I can use as a writer.*
>
> *Was Blanche a 'little person'? Certainly not. She was a demonic creature, the size of her feeling was too great for her to contain without madness.*

> Williams, *Memoirs*, 1976

Tragicomedy, melodrama and soap opera

> *The one American playwright who is a conspicuous exception to the dichotomy between 'high' and 'low' culture is Tennessee Williams. Williams' South, with its sexual ambivalence, self-delusion, and irrational violence, has become part of our popular mythos, the ambience of countless B-movies and television melodramas. Surely, no play of the American theatre, perhaps no play in English since the time of Shakespeare, has won such praise from both the critics and the populace.*

> Kolin in R. C. Small, *A Teacher's Guide to the Signet edition of Tennessee Williams' A Streetcar Named Desire*, 2004

As Kolin suggests here, several of Williams' plays have specific qualities which would seem to belong to the 'lowbrow' popular culture genres of melodrama and soap opera rather than the 'highbrow' elite genre of classical tragedy. Melodramas contain sensational incidents, stereotyped characters, exaggerated emotions and simplistic sentiments, whereas soap operas are often intimate, domestic, family-orientated and theoretically realistic. Relatively few texts share common ground with both *Oedipus the King* and *Game of Thrones*, but several of Williams' key themes – family and sexual politics, greed and betrayal, love and

TASK

While it is perhaps easier to see Blanche as the tragic protagonist of the play, some readers and audiences might prefer to view Stanley as the hero, and in the earlier scenes he does seem more likeable than Blanche. Where do you stand on this key issue, and what textual evidence would you use to support your point of view?

hate, loneliness and death – tap into the perennial concerns important to the audiences who first watched the ancient Greek plays and modern soap addicts alike. Like many of Williams' most memorable characters, Blanche is wrestling with the eternal questions that tortured Oedipus then and now obsess the Starks and the Lanisters. Who are we? How can we find love? What are we here for?

In another of his great plays, *Cat on a Hot Tin Roof* (1955), Williams blended tragic elements such as the haunting suicide of a tormented homosexual and the terminal cancer of the family patriarch Big Daddy with the comically misplaced belief of his sycophantic and super-fertile daughter-in-law Mae that her gruesome squadron of squabbling brats will net her the family fortune. Similarly, in *Streetcar*, Williams juxtaposes diametrically opposed tragic and comic moods in dramatising rape and insanity alongside the domestic squabbling of Blanche and Stanley over her hogging the bathroom and secretly guzzling his whisky. Managing this tragicomic emotional tightrope poses a considerable challenge for actors and audiences alike, yet Williams' skill as a dramatist ensures that the play never descends into cliché or farce as it looks at life in the raw, with all its contradictions and irreconcilabilities.

Social realist drama

The success of *Streetcar* may have been partly due to the new taste for realism that emerged in post-war America; Stanley and Mitch were fellow soldiers and Blanche slept with many young men from the army base near her home in Laurel. Another realistic aspect of the play is its depiction of the rich cultural and racial background of life in working-class New Orleans. At the denouement, virtually all the characters are on stage, from Blanche and Stella with their aristocratic French ancestry to Polish Stanley, Anglo-Irish Mitch, Mexican Pablo and Steve, whose surname, 'Hubbel', suggests he is of German descent. We have also seen the Mexican Woman and the Negro Woman and heard the black musicians playing their jazz and blues.

Streetcar is set just after the seismic upheaval of World War II, and Williams dramatises a remarkable post-war transformation of America in which the economic contribution of men like Stanley will underpin the dawning of a new age of prosperity. The family unit had been split up and threatened during the war years, but afterwards it was seen as the cornerstone of the nation's recovery. Thus popular culture seemed to endorse traditional gender roles by celebrating the domestic responsibilities of women as homemakers and child carers and closing down the alternative possibilities for women which the war had temporarily offered in the absence of men.

▲ Jazz and blues would have provided a vivid soundtrack to life in New Orleans in the 1940s

Morality play

In medieval times, morality plays were didactic texts designed to convey a moral lesson; the characters were allegorical archetypes personifying virtues and vices such as 'Mercy' and 'Greed' in a very schematic manner, with the central theme being mankind's struggle against sin. This explicitly Christian form of theatre was meant to teach the audience about abstract concepts such as virtue, vice and repentance.

Context

The 1946 film *The Best Years of Our Lives* is the story of a soldier, a sailor and an airman trying to readjust to civilian life; a huge critical and commercial success, it won seven Academy Awards. Watch a clip on the internet to get a sense of the challenge to readjust which faced army veterans like Stanley and Mitch after the end of World War II.

Clearly there is plenty of sinning in *Streetcar* – in fact, all the so-called seven deadly sins are represented: wrath, avarice, sloth, pride, lust, envy and gluttony. Yet while punishment is meted out to some (but not all) transgressors, Williams avoids spelling out too schematic a moral message, leaving the moral judgements to his readers and audiences.

TASK

In order to think more deeply about aspects of form and genre, collect evidence of characters committing each of the seven deadly sins in the play. How far do you think it is useful to set a modern play such as *Streetcar* within the framework of a stereotyped medieval drama?

35

Memory play

After World War II, partly influenced by the ideas of psychoanalysts like Sigmund Freud and Carl Jung, the idea of the 'memory play' began to influence a new generation of writers. Williams saw all his major works as 'memory plays' that centre on a character undergoing an intense psychological crisis; this incident is so profound it triggers a time-loop trap during which the trauma must be continuously relived until the character comes to terms with it. Thus the action of the play is non-linear and consciously artificial, with stylised dramatic techniques being used to suggest a psychological or spiritual 'truth' about the inner life of the main protagonist.

Memory plays seek to convey a symbolic truth as opposed to a naturalistic imitation of reality, and it is fascinating to trace those elements of *Streetcar* which seem to conflict with the notion of a 'realistic' text. Williams' use of the Varsouviana to move Blanche in and out of her memories of the past, for instance, adds immeasurably to the audience's understanding of her character even though it is completely artificial. Unlike the other characters on stage, the audience can hear the music that conjures up her remembered experience; in effect Williams has organised the structural framing in which Blanche's memory of Allan's suicide is embedded to minimise our chances of achieving an objective critical stance and encourage us to empathise with her instead. Thus there are effectively two different types of 'reality' operating here, defined by Felicia Hardison Londré as 'the mingling of objective reality and the subjective reality that is seen through the eyes of Blanche DuBois' (Londré in Roudané, 1997). According to Smith-Howard and Heintzelman (2005), the 1947 Broadway production of *Streetcar* was a 'watershed moment in US theatre history. Essentially, Williams created a new genre in the modern theatre: a heightened naturalism that allows dreams (or nightmares) to coexist with reality.'

Taking it further ▶▷

Like *Streetcar*, Arthur Miller's *Death of a Salesman* (1949) uses memories to structure the text in a non-linear way. Miller famously challenges the notion that tragedy must focus upon the downfall of a great man: the hero, Willy Loman, is an ordinary 'low' man. Read *Death of a Salesman* and compare and contrast the ways in which Williams and Miller use memory to emphasise their major themes.

Structure

When we talk about the structure of a play, we mean the manner in which it is put together. At A-level you need to understand the ways in which the structural methods used by the writer contribute to and influence our understanding of the text as a whole.

The structure of *Streetcar* is reminiscent of the Russian playwright Anton Chekhov's famous tragicomedy *The Cherry Orchard* (1903). Both plays deal with the annihilation of a genteel rural aristocratic way of life by a rising and brashly confident lower class, and begin with an arrival and end with a departure. Moreover, like Chekhov, Williams often uses music and sound effects to heighten dramatic tension.

The arrival of the intruder

Like so many plays, *Streetcar* utilises elements of the classical dramatic structure of crisis and climax. The bare bones of the piece fit numerous other plays in which the on-stage action is set in motion by the arrival of an intruder who invades and disrupts an apparently stable and harmonious world before being expelled, whereupon harmony is (more or less) re-established.

The 11 'scenes'

Unlike most plays, which are divided into acts and scenes, Williams chose to structure *A Streetcar Named Desire* into 11 scenes which trace the development of the relationships between Blanche, Stanley and Stella over a few months. The original stage production placed the two intervals after Scene IV (the poker night) and Scene VI (Blanche's date with Mitch) and it has been suggested that this model effectively divides the play into three sections plus a coda, like this:

- **Scenes I–IV**, set in early May, establish a mood of dark comedy.
- **Scenes V and VI**, set on a swelteringly hot August evening, are melancholic, nostalgic and romantic.
- **Scenes VII–X**, set on the afternoon and evening of Blanche's birthday, 15 September, are powerfully dramatic, climactic and tragic.

Then **Scene XI**, set *'some weeks later'*, presumably in the early autumn, works as a kind of desolate tragic coda.

Movement in time

Whereas the onstage action keeps moving forward until Stanley rapes Blanche, we are also taken backwards in time to Blanche's primal sexual trauma, the discovery of Allan's homosexuality and his subsequent suicide. When Blanche finally describes this event to Mitch, years after it took place, it has entirely changed its 'meaning'; at the time she was shocked, appalled and disgusted, but now she feels guilt, sorrow and remorse. Significantly the play begins in the spring and ends in the 'fall'.

Dramatic climaxes

Another notable structural feature is Williams' decision to end each of the 11 scenes with a vivid punchline, startling tableau or arresting visual image. Note the patterned and repetitive nature of these startlingly dramatic closing moments:

- **Scene I** – Blanche sinks down, puts her head in her hands and announces she is going to be sick.

Build critical skills

According to the Greek philosopher Aristotle, the three classical *unities* (rules for drama) are *unity of action*: a play should track one main plot, with no (or few) subplots; *unity of place*: the action should take place in one location; and *unity of time*: the action should take place within a single day. Analyse the ways in which Williams breaks all these 'rules' and comment on what he has gained by doing so.

▼ **Scene II** – Blanche asks: 'Which way do we – go now – Stella? . . . The blind are – leading the blind!' (pages 23–24). The *'blue piano'* and the *'hot trumpet'* are heard.

▼ **Scene III** – Mitch comforts Blanche who declares: 'Thank you for being so kind! I need kindness now' (page 34).

▼ **Scene IV** – Stella embraces Stanley as he grins at Blanche in triumph; the *'blue piano'*, trumpet and drums are heard.

▼ **Scene V** – Blanche kisses the Young Man and gets rid of him only just in time for Mitch's arrival, whereupon she launches into her Southern belle act to dazzle him.

▼ **Scene VI** – Blanche and Mitch embrace at the end of their date and Blanche declares: 'Sometimes – there's God – so quickly!' (page 57).

▼ **Scene VII** – Blanche realises something has gone badly wrong and when Stella denies anything has happened she shouts: 'You're lying! Something has!' As she and Stella freeze, *'The distant piano goes into a hectic breakdown'* (page 63).

▼ **Scene VIII** – Stella goes into labour and as the Varsouviana plays, Blanche sings the Mexican folk-song *'El pan de mais'*.

▼ **Scene IX** – After Mitch attempts to rape her, Blanche screams: 'Fire! Fire! Fire!' and falls to her knees. *'The distant piano is slow and blue'* (page 75).

▼ **Scene X** – Stanley attacks Blanche, declaring: **'We've had this date with each other from the beginning!'** *'She sinks to her knees. He picks up her inert figure and carries her to the bed. The hot trumpet and drums from the Four Deuces sound loudly'* (page 81).

▼ **Scene XI** — Stella weeps in Stanley's arms and as her *'luxurious sobbing'* and his *'sensual murmur'* fade the *'blue piano'* and the *'muted trumpet'* are heard as Steve announces: *'This game is seven-card stud'* (page 90).

Top ten quotation ⇨

Interestingly it is in Scene VI – which comes right at the heart of the play as the middle point of the 11 scenes – that Blanche tells Mitch about the suicide of Allan Grey, the defining event of her life. In terms of some of the key moments or events characteristic of classical tragedy, the **crisis** may be identified as Blanche's decision to reveal the truth about her past to Mitch (Scene IX), the **climax** as her rape by Stanley (Scene X) and the **denouement** her removal to the asylum (Scene XI). Above all, however, it is important to note that the episodic, impressionistic structure of the text allows Williams to reveal crucial snippets of information about Blanche's past scene by scene, thus heightening the dramatic tension. *Streetcar's* structure is thus much looser than that of *Cat on a Hot Tin Roof*, which Williams felt was his most skilfully constructed play in observing the unities of time, place and action. The on-stage action of *Cat on a Hot Tin Roof* plays out in real time, as a highly dysfunctional family goes into meltdown, squabbling over a $10 million fortune and '28,000 acres of the richest land this side of the valley Nile'. (Refer back to page 34 for more detail on *Cat on a Hot Tin Roof*.)

Aspects of setting and staging

In purely theatrical terms, Williams' radical rethinking of how to use the stage space was seen as particularly innovative when the play was first performed. In allowing the audience to witness the events taking place both in the Kowalskis' small cramped flat and the pulsing urban jungle of the Vieux Carré outside, he juxtaposed the realistic and the symbolic in a way which came to be seen as one of his signature dramatic techniques. According to Thomas Adler:

> *Williams fully utilized the stylistic possibilities of the stage ... to break away from the language-bound realistic drama of the nineteenth century ... This new type of play would not only admit but insist that the language of drama involves more than just words; it would acknowledge the stage symbols and the scenic images that speak to the audience as powerfully as what issues from the mouths of the characters.*
>
> Adler in Small, 2004

In *Streetcar* the cramped flat is the arena for combat as Blanche and Stanley fight for physical space and emotional territory with all their associated connotations of invasion and defence, attraction and repulsion. Because Blanche has to sleep on a collapsible put-you-up camp bed it is suggested from the outset that she will be merely passing through Elysian Fields on her journey towards her final destination, Cemeteries; meanwhile the fact that her sleeping quarters are only cordoned off by a flimsy curtain represents her ominous lack of security and protection when living under Stanley's roof.

Stage directions

Tennessee Williams was committed to a form of theatre that aimed to do something other than represent reality in as lifelike a way as possible; he wanted to combine as many of the stage arts as he could to create a theatrical experience greater than the sum of its parts. Thus we have in *Streetcar* theatrical stage directions that seem at once lyrical, symbolic, metaphoric and almost poetic. It is important to recognise the extent to which Williams was an experimental dramatist consciously trying out different styles in order, he felt, to liberate a higher form of psychological truth than a faithful representation of 'real life'. The language of *Streetcar*'s stage directions is an arresting and highly significant aspect of the text that often functions as an extended narrative commentary on key elements of theme and character. In Scene I, for example, Blanche's arrival in the Quarter is described like this:

> *Blanche comes around the corner, carrying a valise. She looks at a slip of paper, then at the building, then again at the slip and again at the building. Her expression is one of shocked disbelief. Her appearance is incongruous to this setting. She is daintily dressed in a white suit with a fluffy bodice, necklace and earrings of pearl,*

white gloves and hat, looking as if she were arriving at a summer tea or cocktail party in the garden district. She is about five years older than Stella. Her delicate beauty must avoid a strong light. There is something about her uncertain manner, as well as her white clothes, that suggests a moth.

It is possible to split up this lengthy passage into three distinct sections. In the first part, Williams provides what we might see as fairly typical stage directions that inform the actor playing the role of Blanche of specific gestures and movements – checking that she has the right address and looking startled when she realises that it is in fact correct. Next comes the part in which Williams describes Blanche's stage costume; here he presents her ladylike 'Southern Belle' outfit as symbolic of her outsider status; what might be perfect for a cocktail party in the upscale garden district is utterly wrong for the Quarter. The ironic symbolism of the white clothes, with their connotations of purity and innocence, will be picked up later when Blanche unpacks her trunk and declares 'Clothes are my passion'. Then in the final couple of lines Williams moves into a lyrical, almost dreamy description of her as a fluttering moth frightened of (and of course fatally drawn to) harsh bright light. While manifestly impossible to actually transfer onto the stage, nonetheless the last section provides a perfect character sketch for the actor and director.

Let's now turn to Williams' keynote description of Stanley at the end of Scene I. While this is not the first occasion on which the audience has seen him, it is deliberately placed directly before his first encounter with Blanche. Pairing and comparing these initial descriptions of the two main characters enables us to see how the playwright has positioned them as adversaries from the outset:

More laughter and shouts of parting come from the men. Stanley throws the screen door of the kitchen open and comes in. He is of medium height, about five feet eight or nine, and strongly, compactly built. Animal joy in his being is implicit in all his movements and attitude. Since earliest manhood the centre of his life has been pleasure with women, the giving and taking of it, not with weak indulgence, dependently, but with the power and pride of a richly feathered male bird among hens. Branching out from this complete and satisfying centre are all the auxiliary channels of his life, such as his heartiness with men, his appreciation of rough humour, his love of good drink and food and games, his car, his radio, everything that is his, that bears his emblem of the gaudy seed-bearer. He sizes up women at a glance, with sexual classifications, crude images flashing into his mind and determining the way he smiles at them.

Once again we see Williams' use of stage directions here to emphasise critical aspects of Stanley's typically 'alpha male' personality and motivation. He has an impressive physical presence and his confident – possibly arrogant – pleasure in his ability to attract women is the cornerstone of his entire personality. His '*power and pride*' provides a direct contrast with Blanche's 'uncertain manner' and the brilliantly coloured clothes he so enjoys wearing cohere with this early description of him as a peacock – surely the 'richly feathered male bird among hens' to which Williams is referring. Stanley is presented as materialistic through the listing of the desirable consumer commodities he owns and enjoys. The implication is that in addition to '*his car*' and '*his radio*', he cherishes his wife. Stella can surely be seen as his ultimate prized possession and linked with the phrase '*everything that is his*', since the fact that she is pregnant with his child means that she literally '*bears his emblem of the gaudy seed-bearer*'. The final sentence emphasises his dominating and threatening masculinity in terms which seem deliberately unsettling and menacing. Indeed Williams follows his depiction of Stanley '*siz[ing] up women at a glance, with sexual classifications, crude images flashing into his mind and determining the way he smiles at them*' with a stage direction that clearly suggests that Blanche picks up on this implicit sexual threat, '*drawing back involuntarily from his stare*'.

The play's most iconic scene description comes at the beginning of Scene III, 'The Poker Night'. The striking stage directions here are classic Williams, demonstrating the key features of his signature flamboyance:

The Poker Night.

There is a picture of Van Gogh's of a billiard parlour at night. The kitchen now suggests that sort of lurid nocturnal brilliance, the raw colours of childhood's spectrum. Over the yellow linoleum of the kitchen table hangs an electric bulb with a vivid green glass shade. The poker players – Stanley, Steve, Mitch and Pablo – wear coloured shirts, solid blues, a purple, a red-and-white check, a light green, and they are men at the peak of their physical manhood, as coarse and direct and powerful as the primary colours. There are vivid slices of watermelon on the table, whisky bottles and glasses. The bedroom is relatively dim with only the light that spills between the portières and through the wide window on the street.

For a moment there is absorbed silence as a hand is dealt.

The startlingly rich and intense colour palette here – yellow, green, purple, blue and red – is a world away from Blanche's defining white, while the '*lurid nocturnal brilliance*' and vivid rawness of the lighting bodes ill for a character who was explicitly likened to a '*moth*' whose '*delicate beauty must avoid a strong light*' in Scene I. Thus it is possible to see Williams' powerfully evocative stage directions arcing across from scene to scene to provide a sense of narrative continuity for the reader as well as very clear directions for the lighting and set designers working on a new stage production. In summary, Williams' idiosyncratic and instantly recognisable descriptive stage directions go well beyond 'exit stage left' to function as an omniscient narrative viewpoint very unusual in drama. This aspect of his stagecraft makes *Streetcar*, like most of his other plays, almost as rewarding to encounter as a reader as to experience in performance.

Taking it further ▶

Tennessee Williams called an earlier draft of the play 'The Poker Night', which underlines the crucial significance of this scene. The stage directions refer to an 1888 painting by the Dutch Expressionist artist Vincent Van Gogh called *The Night Café*. Have a look at this painting online.

▲ Two key sound effects feature in the play: the blue piano and the Varsouviana

Sound effects

As well as his beautiful and unusual scenic descriptions, Williams' use of sound is equally rich, symbolic and non-naturalistic. As well as realistic sound effects that signal the ongoing passage of everyday life – the loud rattling of a train passing across the railway tracks, for instance, or the water running for one of Blanche's endless baths, or the shrill piercing of a policeman's whistle – Williams uses artificial sound effects to enhance the atmosphere or heighten the audience's awareness of the psychological states of his characters. The key sound effects that feature in the play are the blue piano and the Varsouviana, two very different types of music that evoke both Blanche's new surroundings and her tragic past.

The blue piano

The blue piano is the sound of the Dixieland jazz emanating from the Four Deuces in the Vieux Carré. For Stanley, Stella, Steve and Eunice this local bar represents the vibrant, joyful, working-class culture of multicultural New Orleans; thus on one level this sound effect is naturalistic, because it conjures up the essence of everyday life. On another level, however, the distinctive bluesy jazz soundtrack seems to cohere with the ups and downs of the protagonists' lives in a highly symbolic and suggestive manner. For instance, when Blanche refuses to believe Stella's assurance that Mitch's failure to appear at her birthday tea is nothing to worry about, the stage directions are hugely significant; *'She stares fearfully at Stella, who pretends to be busy at the table. The distant piano goes into a hectic breakdown'.* The implication here must be that the music is fragmenting along with Blanche's hopes for a secure future with Mitch and echoing her imminent psychological collapse. Later, when Stanley assaults Blanche, his aggressively dominating physical actions are underscored and reinforced by the brassy jazz of the blue piano; *'He picks up her inert figure and carries her to the bed. The hot trumpet and drums from the Four Deuces sound loudly'.*

The Varsouviana

The Varsouviana polka music is the most famous stage effect in the play and can be seen as typical of Williams' flamboyant dramatic style. As a playwright determined to make use of the broadest possible range of dramatic techniques, he remained true to his conception of a distinctive 'plastic theatre' which would incorporate expressionist features to reflect the psychology of his characters, which is precisely what the Varsouviana does for Blanche. Unlike the 'blue piano' music which is designed to suggest the atmosphere of New Orleans while often also reflecting and enhancing elements of character or moments of rising dramatic tension, the Varsouviana is an artificial sound effect heard only in Blanche's imagination and by no other characters on stage.

The polka tune symbolises her husband's suicide, the tragic event which wrecked Blanche's life; hearing it sends her into an extreme state of panic and fear which only ends when she hears the climactic and terrible sound of a gunshot. Williams' use of the Varsouviana to move Blanche in and out of her memories of the past adds immeasurably to the audience's understanding of her character and is the key element of *Streetcar* which challenges the notion of a 'realistic' text, being deliberately stylised, expressionist and artificial. Unlike the other characters on stage, the audience can, of course, hear the music that conjures up her remembered experience; in effect, Williams uses the polka tune as a framework for Blanche's memory of Allan's suicide to encourage us to empathise with his tragic heroine. Yet as the dramatic action develops, Williams can be seen to use this sound effect in subtly different ways to predict Blanche's tragic future as well as to resurrect her past. It is therefore very important to review the different instances of the Varsouviana that occur throughout the play.

At the very end of the first scene, Stanley casually mentions Blanche's dead husband – 'You were married once, weren't you?' Instantly *the music of the polka rises up, faint in the distance.* When she admits 'The boy – the boy died', the stage directions indicate *She sinks back down before muttering*, 'I'm afraid I'm – going to be sick!'. By closing the scene on this starkly memorable tableau, Williams has skilfully alerted the audience to the importance of the polka tune while leaving them in suspense as to its full significance.

It is at the very end of Scene VI, after their unsuccessful date, that the full significance of the Varsouviana is revealed to the audience as Blanche tells Mitch about the night Allan died. Following her accidental discovery of her young husband with another man, she explains how the fateful evening unwound to its horrific conclusion:

> **Blanche:** Afterwards we pretended that nothing had been discovered. Yes, the three of us drove out to Moon Lake Casino, very drunk and laughing all the way.
>
> *Polka music sounds, in a minor key faint with distance.*

TASK

Consider how far you feel it is significant, given Stanley's ethnicity, that Varsouviana means 'from Warsaw' (the capital of Poland) and that this polka was originally a Polish peasant dance. Think about why Williams chose this simple, sentimental tune to express such heightened and complex emotions. You can listen to it being played on YouTube by searching for 'Varsouviana County Fair'.

We danced the Varsouviana! Suddenly in the middle of the dance the boy I had married broke away from me and ran out of the casino. A few moments later – a shot!

The Polka stops abruptly.

Blanche rises stiffly. Then the Polka resumes in a major key.

I ran out – all did! – all ran and gathered about the terrible thing at the edge of the lake! I couldn't get near for the crowding. Then someone caught my arm. 'Don't go any closer! Come back! You don't want to see! See? See what! Then I heard voices say – Allan! Allan! The Grey boy! He'd stuck a revolver into his mouth, and fired – so that the back of his head had been – blown away!

She stops and covers her face.

It was because – on the dance-floor – unable to stop myself – I'd suddenly said – 'I know! I know! You disgust me …' And then the searchlight which had been turned on in the world was turned off again and never for one moment since has there been any light that's stronger than this – kitchen – candle …

Mitch gets up awkwardly and moves towards her a little. The Polka music increases. Mitch stands beside her.

Mitch: [*drawing her slowly into his arms*]: You need somebody. And I need somebody too. Could it be – you and me, Blanche?

She stares at him vacantly for a moment. Then with a soft cry huddles in his embrace. She makes a sobbing effort to speak but the words won't come. He kisses her forehead and her eyes and finally her lips. The Polka tune fades out. Her breath is drawn and released in long, grateful sobs.

Blanche: Sometimes – there's God – so quickly!

The richness and complexity of Williams' dramaturgy is shown in his merging of aural and verbal symbolism; as the Varsouviana polka music plays in the background to externalise the memory of Allan's death, Blanche tells Mitch how falling in love had illuminated her world with a 'blinding light' which was brutally extinguished when he killed himself. The impact on Mitch is powerful, as having heard the tragic story of Allan's death and seeing for himself Blanche's extreme distress, he finds the confidence to offer her comfort. This point in the play is in fact the high-water mark of Blanche's fortunes, as the scene closes on the two lonely souls clasping each other and seemingly united in an attempt to console each other for their grief and loss. The Varsouviana continues to play as

Blanche huddles in his embrace as if it may take on a new significance as the mood music for a potential healing process, although the next scene, of course, makes it clear that this can never be. Crucially, from this dramatic midpoint onwards the audience is fully aware of the polka tune's symbolic function as an index or signifier for Blanche's psychological state.

In Scene VIII, Williams employs the Varsouviana to foreshadow Blanche's own sexual annihilation as opposed to reviving the memory of Allan's. The parallels between Blanche's accusation of Allan and her rape by Stanley were explicitly linked as far back as Scene II, in another example of Williams' brilliant use of proleptic irony. When Stanley roughly grabs hold of Allan's poems and love letters, Blanche instinctively recognises the threat he poses, saying 'I hurt him the way you would like to hurt me'. Here it is Stanley's malicious gift of a bus ticket back to Laurel that initiates the sound effect of the polka tune, as opposed to anything Blanche herself does:

> *The Varsouviana music steals in softly and continues playing. Stella rises abruptly and turns her back. Blanche tries to smile. Then she tries to laugh. Then she gives both up and springs from the table and runs into the next room. She clutches her throat and then runs into the bathroom. Coughing, gagging sounds are heard.*

As in Scene I, the polka tune is linked here with Blanche feeling physically sick due to her isolation and vulnerability to Stanley's menace. At the end of this scene, with Blanche still offstage, the Varsouviana is heard as Stella, who has gone into labour, leaves for the hospital:

> *He is with her now, supporting her with his arm, murmuring indistinguishably as they go outside. The 'Varsouviana' is heard, its music rising with sinister rapidity as the bathroom door opens slightly. Blanche comes out twisting a washcloth. She begins to whisper the words as the light fades slowly.*

As the scene ends, with Blanche ominously alone in the Kowalskis' apartment for the very first time, she whispers the simple words of a Mexican folk song, 'El Pan de Mais' (Maize Bread) as if the significance of the Varsouviana is fading. No longer linked solely with the death of Allan Grey, the polka tune now presages another defining crisis in Blanche's life.

Scene IX opens on a tableau in which Williams spells out the new duality of the Varsouviana in resurrecting the past and foretelling the future and reveals Blanche's frightening mental deterioration:

> *Blanche is seated in a tense hunched position in a bedroom chair that she has re-covered with diagonal green and white stripes. She has on her scarlet satin robe. On the table beside the chair is a bottle of liquor and a glass. The rapid, feverish polka tune, the*

'Varsouviana', is heard. The music is in her mind; she is drinking to escape it and the sense of disaster closing in on her, and she seems to whisper the words of the song.

With the arrival of Mitch, *'the polka tune stops'* but as she realises the depth of his anger, Blanche begins to voice her experience of the Varsouviana aloud. In theatrical terms, Williams' signature sound effect has now become something that his characters discuss openly in another remarkable instance of his experimental dramatic approach:

Blanche: You've stopped that polka tune that I had caught in my head. Have you ever had anything caught in your head? Some words, a piece of music? That goes relentlessly on and on in your head? No, of course you haven't, you dumb angel-puss, you'd never get anything awful caught in your head!

As Mitch continues to show his anger and bitterness, Blanche resorts to her usual modus operandi of play-acting and pretence:

Blanche: Something's the matter tonight, but never mind. I won't cross-examine the witness. I'll just – *[She touches her forehead vaguely. The polka tune starts up again.]* – pretend I don't notice anything different about you! That – music again …

Mitch: What music?

Blanche: The 'Varsouviana'? The polka tune they were playing when Allan – Wait!

A distant revolver shot is heard, Blanche seems relieved.

There now, the shot! It always stops after that.

The polka music dies out again.

Yes, now it's stopped.

Mitch: Are you boxed out of your mind?

Later in this scene, at the appearance of the sinister Mexican Woman selling flowers for the dead, *the polka tune fades in* again. The eerie and haunting cry of *'Flores para los muertos'* triggers a sequence of terrible memories for Blanche, who tells Mitch of the family illnesses and deaths that she tried to compensate for by an ultimately ruinous series of promiscuous encounters with the young soldiers training at the local army camp. The polka tune is heard onstage throughout her painful 'confession' but as her tale concludes and the Mexican Woman drifts away, so too does the sound of the Varsouviana.

Fittingly it is in the play's final scene when the Varsouviana is heard for the last time. Blanche is waiting with Stella and Eunice for the arrival of a visitor whom she believes to be her old beau Shep Huntleigh. In fact, of course, the man coming to take her away is a doctor from the asylum. As she awaits her doom, *the 'Varsouviana' faintly plays,* suggesting the jumble of past trauma and present horror that exists inside her mind. When she finally sees the doctor and realises that he is a stranger *the 'Varsouviana' is playing distantly.* Williams uses the polka tune for the last time to externalise the fragmentation of Blanche's sense of self as Stanley '*suddenly pulls back his chair and rises as if to block her way'* in a physical gesture that evokes the horror of the night he raped her:

> *She rushes past him into the bedroom. Lurid reflections appear on the walls in odd, sinuous shapes. The 'Varsouviana' is filtered into weird distortion, accompanied by the cries and noises of the jungle. Blanche seizes the back of a chair as if to defend herself.*

The ultimate '*distortion*' of the polka tune and the way in which it is overlaid by the cries of the jungle vividly suggests that Blanche's mind has given way, brutalised and ruined at last by Stanley. From the first scene to the last, then, Williams makes the fullest possible use of the Varsouviana to dramatise his heroine's interior life and cue the audience into her complex psychology.

Lighting effects

Lighting cues are often employed to create dramatic tension or emphasise a key aspect of a character's emotional state. At the end of Scene IV, for instance, when Stanley grins at Blanche in triumph, knowing that Stella has rejected her sister's proposed escape plan, '*as the lights fade away, with a lingering brightness on their embrace, the music of the "blue piano" and trumpet and drums are heard'.* The image of husband and wife clinging together in silhouette as the stage lights fade strongly indicates their indissoluble union. At the beginning of Scene VIII, which centres on Blanche's abortive birthday party, the lighting effects are extremely suggestive:

> *The view through the big windows is fading gradually into a still-golden dusk. A torch of sunlight blazes on the side of a big water-tank or oil-drum across the empty lot toward the business district which is now pierced by pin-points of lighted windows or windows reflecting the sunset.*

The lighting cues here achieve several important effects. As the second of the four scenes that take place on the afternoon and evening of 15 September, Williams uses the dying afternoon sunshine here to denote that Blanche's hopes of Mitch's arrival are fading along with the light. In practical terms the decline of the day towards 'sunset' indicates the day's ongoing timeline of events, while also symbolically representing the slow death of all her dreams. In terms of the

Build critical skills

Select and analyse another of Williams' uses of lighting cues in the play. How does he employ the visual effects of light to emphasise certain aspects of setting, staging, plot or characterisation?

language with which Williams chooses to describe the lighting here, one might see the image of harsh light bouncing starkly off an ugly metallic object within a bleak industrial landscape as somewhat repellent, and the verbs '*blazes*' and '*pierced*' as connoting violent aggression. The arresting final image of '*lighted windows or windows reflecting the sunset*' may be seen to suggest the myriad other stories of personal triumph and tragedy that could be going on behind those other windows picked out by the dying light of day. Perhaps Blanche's story is just one human tragedy among many.

The interior and the exterior

The fact that the street outside the Kowalskis' cramped apartment is also visible to the audience implies that the home offers scant protection from the wider world. Other places mentioned but never seen remind us of further aspects of the characters' lives – the bowling alley and the Four Deuces provide an index for Stanley's macho working-class world just as Belle Reve, the Moon Lake Casino and the Flamingo Hotel are the staging posts for Blanche's downfall. The interface between these inside and outside spaces suggests the apartment is a liminal or threshold place rather than a safe haven. At the climax of Scene X, one of the play's most startling dramatic effects is seen:

> [Blanche] sets the phone down and crosses warily into the kitchen.
>
> The night is filled with inhuman voices like cries in a jungle.
>
> The shadows and lurid reflections move sinuously as flames along the wall spaces.
>
> Through the back wall of the rooms, which have become transparent, can be seen the sidewalk. A prostitute has rolled a drunkard. He pursues her along the walk, overtakes her and there is a struggle. A policeman's whistle breaks it up. The figures disappear.
>
> Some moments later the Negro Woman appears around the corner with a sequined bag which the prostitute had dropped on the walk. She is rooting excitedly through it.
>
> Blanche presses her knuckles to her lips and returns slowly to the phone. She speaks in a hoarse whisper.

Just before Stanley rapes Blanche, therefore, the back wall separating the Kowalskis' apartment from the world outside disappears and Williams presents what is in effect a brief 'play within a play'. This unusual expressionist effect allows the playwright to give the audience a glimpse of the feral, febrile, brutal violence occurring out on the street; a sexually promiscuous woman has robbed an alcohol-soaked client and he chases after her to gain his revenge. Luckily for her, there is an officer of the law around to prevent a full-blown attack.

Context

Shakespeare's *Hamlet* (c1599-1602) contains the most famous example of a 'play-within-a-play' ever written. Hamlet asks some strolling players to perform a play he calls 'The Mousetrap' in order to expose his uncle's murder of Hamlet's father, telling himself 'the play's the thing,/Wherein I'll catch the conscience of the king'. In *Streetcar*, the tableau of the prostitute, the drunk and the Negro Woman dramatises a minor crime while foreshadowing (as opposed to mirroring) a worse one.

The outbreak of violence between these sketchy male and female figures – who clearly resemble stereotypical aspects of the characters of Blanche and Stanley – prefigures the personal violation about to happen inside the apartment shortly thereafter, with no one around to prevent it. The final appearance of the Negro Woman, caring nothing for the prostitute's misfortune and eager to profit from her loss, suggests the dog-eat-dog ethos that pervades here.

Metatheatre

Metatheatre is a self-conscious awareness in a play of its status as a theatrical performance. Such awareness can work through the persistent use of theatrical images, metaphors, or through more overt structural devices such as a 'play within the play'. Blanche is from the start a woman in disguise who orchestrates a range of theatrical performances to cover up the reality she cannot bear to face. In *Streetcar* there are a number of important metatheatrical references, images and elements that contribute to the overall structural cohesion of the text:

- When Blanche first arrives at Elysian Fields, she is described as '*daintily dressed in a white suit with a fluffy bodice, necklace and earrings of pearl, white gloves and hat, looking as if she were arriving at a summer tea or cocktail party in the garden district*'. She is, in other words, inappropriately costumed for this context.

- Blanche's trunk of clothes may be seen as a kind of dressing-up box in which she stores the costumes she needs in order to perform her chosen roles. Stanley sees this clearly, asking Stella: 'What is this sister of yours, a deep-sea diver who brings up sunken treasures? Or is she the champion safe cracker of all time?'. Crucially but accurately, Stanley sums up her life in Laurel as 'the same old lines, same old act, same old hooey'. Later he taunts her with her efforts to create an appropriate 'setting' in which to perform:

- **'You come in here and sprinkle the place with powder and spray perfume and cover the light-bulb with a paper lantern, and lo and behold the place has turned into Egypt and you are the Queen of the Nile!'**

  > Top ten quotation

- Mitch is Blanche's admiring audience in Scene III as she uses music and choreography to create her illusions and maintains her performance throughout Scenes V and VI. Once Stanley has told Mitch about Blanche's past, it is sheer outrage at the gap between the ladylike spinster schoolmarm role she has been playing all summer for his benefit and the sordid truth about the Flamingo Hotel that provokes him to violence in Scene IX.

- In Scene I Stanley removes his vest in front of Blanche, which is clearly inappropriate as well as offering an implied sexual threat, while his gaudy bowling shirt signals his brash and competitive nature. When he appears wearing the silk pyjamas he bought for his wedding night with Stella, his costume seems to suggest that his rape of her sister is predestined.

- At the start of Scene X Blanche is described as having '*decked herself out in a somewhat soiled and crumpled white satin evening gown and a pair*

TASK

There are frequent references to acting and performance throughout the play, such as 'make-believe' and 'putting on an act'. Working either on your own or with a partner, collect as many other instances of metatheatre as possible and analyse the ways in which this technique may shed light on Williams' themes and characters.

of scuffed silver slippers . . . she is placing the rhinestone tiara on her head before the mirror of the dressing-table and murmuring excitedly as if to a group of spectral admirers'. In effect she is presented as an actress putting the final touches to her costume before going on stage.

▼ Williams makes use of a non-naturalistic tableau or mini 'play within a play' with the interpolated vignette of the prostitute, the drunk and the Negro Woman in Scene X.

▼ In Scene XI Blanche is dressed first in a '*red satin robe*', which connotes sexuality, before changing into a jacket of 'Della Robbia blue. The blue of the robe in the old Madonna pictures'. Symbolically she may be seen as shedding the costume (and hence the role) of the 'scarlet woman' here and adopting instead the persona of the Holy Virgin. As she talks to Stella and Eunice, she is hidden behind the 'portières' – full-length curtains which serve to divide the living space. In effect, Blanche is seen to be waiting for the curtain to rise on her final performance in the Kowalskis' apartment.

▲ Vivien Leigh as Blanche and Marlon Brando as Stanley in Elia Kazan's film version of *A Streetcar Named Desire* in 1951

Context

In *Cat on a Hot Tin Roof*, Williams describes the Pollitt mansion as '*Victorian with a touch of the Far East*', thus neatly encapsulating that play's uneasy juxtaposition of foreign, erotic and exotic elements and stifling conservative morality. In *Streetcar* the 'epic fornications' indulged in by Blanche's and Stella's DuBois ancestors seem glaringly out of context when set against the beauty of Belle Reve in its prime.

Binary opposites

The concept of binary opposites stems from the work of the French intellectuals Claude Lévi-Strauss (1908–2009) and Roland Barthes (1915–80), who were closely associated with the theory of structuralism.

In terms of literary theory, structuralists argue that since the meaning of a word is not actually contained in its name, we tend to construct its meaning by relating each word to its opposite. They characterise words as symbols which signify society's ideas and suggest that meaning emerges from the 'gap' between two opposing concepts; thus in order to grasp an idea such as masculinity, we refer to its binary opposite, femininity. Layers of inferential meaning can emerge when a writer consciously structures a text using core oppositions and patterns like this, and in *Streetcar* Williams makes frequent use of this technique by inviting his readers and audiences to consider such dichotomies, particularly as embodied by Stanley and Blanche:

- ❍ masculinity and femininity
- ❍ birth and death
- ❍ regeneration and decay
- ❍ materialism and idealism
- ❍ physicality and spirituality
- ❍ new and old
- ❍ present and past
- ❍ fertility and sterility
- ❍ bold colour and white light.

CRITICAL VIEW

Structuralism has been defined as the search for the underlying patterns of thought in all aspects of human life; it involves comparing the relationships between elements in any given system.

Williams often places similar or contrasting ideas or concepts close together to shed light on them both. Consider Williams' reasons for using the structural techniques of **juxtapositioning**, **patterning** and **doubling** in the following examples:

- ❍ The first half of the play is dominated by Stanley, who generally gets most sympathy from the audience here; this is reversed in the latter stages as we come to transfer our sympathies to Blanche.
- ❍ Blanche queens it over the bathroom; Stanley's poker buddies throw him into the shower to sober up.
- ❍ Blanche sings 'Paper Moon' in the bathroom while Stanley tells Stella the truth about her sister's life behind Blanche's back.
- ❍ Blanche discusses Hawthorne, Whitman, Poe and Browning with Mitch (Scene III) while Stella reads 'a book of coloured comics' in Scene IV just before Blanche tries to appeal to her to recognise 'art', 'poetry' and 'music' as necessary for a civilised life.
- ❍ Stanley removes his vest in front of Blanche while she asks him to zip up the back of her dress.
- ❍ Stanley rifles through Blanche's trunk; she steals his whisky and hides the evidence.

- The choric figures darken; first we hear the tamale seller with his 'red hots'; later it is the Mexican Woman selling her flowers for the dead.
- Both Stanley and Blanche are shown as hardened heavy drinkers; but he is free to drink with his poker buddies in public, the social mores of the genteel Old South mean she has to lie about her drinking and keep it secret.

Foreshadowing

Foreshadowing, sometimes referred to as proleptic irony, is a method of providing structural cohesion by dropping hints to the audience that help them to predict future events. Williams makes much use of this technique:

- In Scene I, Stanley throws a package of meat for Stella to catch, which Eunice and the Negro Woman find highly amusing; they have clearly decoded the sexual innuendo behind his macho gesture. In hurling the meat Stanley signals his sexual domination over her and in catching it, Stella reveals the depth of her sexual obsession with him.
- Stanley's metaphorical rape of Blanche's trunk, jewellery and love-letters, plus Mitch's botched assault on her, prefigure the climax of the play.
- Stanley's 'breakdown' during the poker night, which involves him being overwhelmed against his will by his friends, foreshadows Blanche's breakdown and forcible restraint before she is taken to the asylum.
- Blanche's kissing the Young Man foreshadows the revelation that she was sacked for seducing her student.

Language

Language in *Streetcar* taps into a wide range of dramatic effects. Thus, for example, the following section discusses stage directions – which are obviously not part of the experience of an audience in the theatre in written form – in order to stress that 'language' in this play needs to be seen as more than simply words or dialogue, but as an integral part of Williams' overarching 'plastic theatre' experience.

The play's title

Williams was a genius at signalling the central theme of a text with an evocative metaphorical title which gets straight to the heart of things (see also *Cat on a Hot Tin Roof*) but if the brilliantly sleazy *A Streetcar Named Desire* is not the greatest title ever, it is hard to think of many that can rival it. As Felicia Hardison Londré notes, 'the mundane concreteness of "streetcar" and the abstract quality of aspiration evoked in "desire" point to the many antinomies – thematic, symbolic, and imagistic oppositions – imbedded throughout the play' (Londré in Roudané, 1997). Moreover, the fact that there really were streetcars called Desire and Cemeteries rattling through New Orleans reinforces the real-life context and setting of the play as well as drawing attention to Blanche's fatal journey via Elysian Fields to her symbolic 'death' in the asylum.

TASK

Analyse Williams' purpose in establishing Blanche as a practised drinker who is not above sneaking Stanley's whisky behind his back in Scene I; he comments 'Liquor goes fast in hot weather' as he *holds the bottle to the light to observe its depletion'*. What is the effect on the audience here?

Although he had apparently had *A Streetcar Named Desire* in mind all along, Williams did consider some other potential titles for the play. In 1945 he wrote to his agent, Audrey Wood: 'I have been buried in work the last week or so and am about 55 or 60 pages into the first draft of a play which I am trying to design for [famous American actress Katharine] Cornell. At the moment it has four different titles, *The Moth*, *The Poker Night*, *The Primary Colors*, or *Blanche's Chair in the Moon*. It is about two sisters, the remains of a fallen Southern family. The younger, Stella, has accepted the situation, married beneath her socially and moved to a Southern city with her coarsely attractive, plebeian mate. But Blanche (the Cornell part) has remained at Belle-reve, the home place in ruins, and struggles for five years to maintain the old order' (Williams, *Notebooks*, 2006).

> **TASK**
>
> Consider the possible significance of Williams' four rejected titles and suggest which of the play's themes each seems to encapsulate.

Images, motifs and symbols

Writers often use related language patterns and clusters to infuse certain characters with particular associations, evoke a specific mood or atmosphere, or draw attention to a particularly significant theme. In *Streetcar* Williams uses recurring images, motifs and symbols to create a sense of dramatic and structural coherence and while his symbolism is often verbal (which is why this section has been placed under the AO2 strand of 'language') remember that he interweaves and reinforces these linguistic images with powerfully vivid aural and visual effects. Thus it is important to think about how the overarching effects of Williams' highly wrought, complex images, motifs and symbols enrich the unique atmosphere of the play.

Some of *Streetcar*'s most powerful visual, aural and verbal motifs are listed here:

▼ the coke stain on Blanche's white dress, which symbolises her tarnished past

▼ Blanche's frequent baths, which suggest her wish to cleanse herself

▼ the Chinese paper lantern, which represents Blanche's wish to disguise reality and substitute 'magic'

▼ the streetcar's journey, which connotes sexual passion

▼ Desire and Cemeteries, which connote Blanche's fatal journey and explicitly link sex and death in terms of two types of love characterised by Freud as eros (the desire for life) and thanatos (the longing for oblivion and death)

▼ the Varsouviana, which represents the death of Allan Grey

▼ the blue piano, which evokes the earthy multicultural atmosphere of the Vieux Carré

▼ Blanche and Stanley as symbolic archetypes reflecting a wider cultural debate about the nature of the Old South and the new post-war America.

Animals

▼ Blanche is described as having something about her that suggests a 'moth' (page 5).

▼ Stella describes Stanley to Blanche as of a 'different species' (page 10).

▼ Blanche asks Stella if Mitch is a 'wolf' (page 27).

▼ After Stanley throws the radio out of the window Stella yells: 'Drunk – drunk – animal thing, you!' (page 31).

▼ When he calls for Stella, Stanley is described as '*throw[ing] back his head like a baying hound*' (page 33).

▼ When they make up after their fight Stanley and Stella are said to '*come together with low animal moans*' (page 33).

▼ In her set-piece speech to Stella, Blanche describes Stanley as 'bestial', 'like an animal' and 'ape-like' (pages 40–41).

▼ Stanley mocks Blanche as she sings in the bathroom as 'canary-bird' (pages 59 and 63).

▼ Stella is disgusted by Stanley's table manners and calls him a 'pig' (page 65).

▼ Mitch accuses Blanche of 'lapping it up all summer like a wild-cat!' (page 71).

▼ Blanche renames the Flamingo Hotel the 'Tarantula Arms' and describes herself as 'a big spider! That's where I brought my victims' (page 73).

▼ Blanche talks of 'casting her pearls before swine' to Stanley (page 78).

▼ The outside scene in the Vieux Carré is described as a 'jungle' and '*inhuman voices like cries in a jungle*' are heard (page 79).

▼ Stanley 'springs' at Blanche, calling her 'Tiger – tiger!' in excitement as she tries to fight him off (page 81).

▼ Eunice accuses the men of 'making pigs of yourselves' (page 82).

▼ Blanche wants to wear a brooch shaped like a 'seahorse' (page 82) for her imaginary cruise with Shep Huntleigh.

▼ As Blanche is about to be taken to the asylum, '*cries and noises of the jungle*' are heard (page 87).

▼ When Blanche screams in fear as Stanley tears the lantern down, '*the men spring to their feet*' (pages 87–88).

▼ As the doctor calms Blanche, '*the inhuman cries and noises die out*' (page 89).

▼ Stella '*sobs with inhuman abandon*' after Blanche has been taken away (page 89).

TASK

Analyse these key imagery clusters and assess the ways in which they serve to highlight Williams' themes. If you work with other students here you might allocate one section to each group. Each group might produce a PowerPoint or poster that logs and analyses such instances to present to the rest of the class.

Fire, redness, blood and heat

▼ Blanche uses the word 'bleeding' to describe the suffering of the dying at Belle Reve (page 12).

▼ Blanche emerges from the bathroom '*in a red satin robe*' (page 18).

▼ After Stanley snatches her love-letters from Allan Grey, Blanche declares 'I'll burn them!' (page 22).

▼ Blanche tells Stella that Stanley is 'what we need to mix with our blood now that we've lost Belle Reve' (page 23).

▼ The Mexican tamale vendor calls out 'red hots!' (page 23).

- Stanley complains 'Goddamn, it's hot in here with the steam from the bathroom' (page 67).
- Blanche shouts 'Fire! Fire! Fire!' to scare Mitch away (page 75).
- Stanley tells Blanche it is 'a red letter night for us both' (page 77).
- Blanche appears with '*a tragic radiance in her red satin robe following the sculptural lines of her body*' (page 83).

Water, sea and rain

- Blanche sings 'From the land of the sky blue water/They brought a captive maid' (page 16).
- Stanley asks 'What is this sister of yours, a deep-sea diver who brings up sunken treasures?' (page 18).
- Stanley's card game is called 'Spit in the Ocean' (page 28).
- After his drunken rage on poker night, Stanley says 'I want water' and is thrown into the shower by Mitch (page 32).
- Blanche tells Stella she has sought protection under 'leaky roof[s] . . . because it was storm – all storm' (page 45).
- Blanche asks the Young Man, 'Don't you just love these long rainy afternoons' (page 48).
- Blanche tells Mitch about Allan's suicide and the sight of his dead body, 'the terrible thing at the edge of the lake' (page 57).
- Stanley tells Stella that when Blanche had to leave Laurel she was 'washed up like poison' (page 60).
- Blanche declares after one of her many baths, 'Oh, I feel so good after my long, hot bath, I feel so good and cool and – rested!' (page 63).
- Blanche fantasises about 'taking a swim, a moonlight swim at the old rock-quarry . . . only you've got to be careful to dive where the deep pool is – if you hit a rock you don't come up until tomorrow' (page 75).
- Blanche tells Stanley she is going on 'a cruise of the Caribbean on a yacht' with Shep Huntleigh (page 76).
- Stanley foams up the beer bottle and holds it over his head saying to Blanche, 'Ha-ha! Rain from heaven! . . . Shall we bury the hatchet and make it a loving-cup?' (page 77).
- Blanche asks if the grapes are 'washed'. She declares, 'I can smell the sea air . . . when I die, I'm going to die on the sea . . . And I'll be buried at sea sewn up in a clean white sack and dropped overboard . . . into an ocean as blue as my first lover's eyes!' (pages 84–85).

> **TASK**
>
> In Scene II Blanche is heard singing the sentimental ballad 'From the land of the sky blue water'. The lyrics can be found at http://en.wikipedia.org by searching on 'land sky blue water'. 'In what ways is this song appropriate for Blanche? You might consider:
>
> - her situation in the Kowalskis' flat
> - how it might foreshadow the play's climax
> - ideas of your own.

Light

▼ Blanche's '*delicate beauty must avoid a strong light*' (page 5).

▼ Stella tells Blanche she is 'standing in the light' and is visible through the curtains to the poker players (page 27).

▼ Blanche asks Mitch to place an 'adorable little coloured paper lantern' over the bare bulb in the bedroom (page 30).

▼ Blanche asks the Young Man to light her cigarette (page 48).

▼ Blanche tells Mitch 'I want to create – joie de vivre! I'm lighting a candle' (page 52).

▼ Blanche tells Mitch being in love with Allan Grey was like turning on 'a blinding light' but that since his death 'the searchlight which had been turned on the world was turned off again and never for one moment since has there been any light that's stronger than this – kitchen – candle' (pages 56–57).

▼ Stella lights the candles on Blanche's birthday cake (page 66).

▼ Stanley describes making love with Stella as getting **'them coloured lights going'** (page 68).

Top ten quotation

▼ Mitch forces Blanche into the light and stares at her as she '*cries out and covers her face*' (page 72).

▼ As Blanche is being taken to the asylum, Stanley rips down her paper lantern '*and extends it towards her. She cries out as if the lantern was herself*' (page 87).

Dialogue

Williams is famous for the way he brings his hauntingly memorable characters to life through dialogue which can be realistic, vivid, poetic, tragic, comic – and sometimes all of the above. In Shakespeare's day, blank verse was the usual form of language for characters of a high social rank while common characters often spoke in prose; in *Streetcar*, Blanche's dreamy, educated, high-register language, which incorporates literary references and French and Spanish vocabulary, is a world away from Stanley's colloquial working-class demotic argot. Blanche is an English teacher, so literature is obviously part and parcel of her stock-in-trade, but Williams carefully chooses her authors and references to add extra layers of meaning. Her ability to summon up apt literary allusions and references makes her speech sound very different from that of Stella, who, like Stanley, is much more literal.

Williams' lyrical and beautiful dialogue is one of his most characteristic qualities as a dramatist, although one which he came to feel left him 'dated' later in his career. In the mid-1960s, when his reputation was in decline, he wrote:

My great bête noir[e] as a writer has been a tendency ... to poeticize ... and that's why I suppose I've written so many Southern heroines. They have the tendency to gild the lily, and they speak in a rather florid style which seems to suit me because I write out of emotion, and I get carried away by emotion.

Williams, 2006

In *Streetcar*, however, when he was at the peak of his dramatic powers, his dialogue was (and still is) seen as one of the greatest strengths of the play. The critic Alfred Uhry has suggested that *A Streetcar Named Desire* 'contains the finest dialogue ever written for an American play'.

The four main characters are very clearly differentiated by their dialogue. Blanche's language includes artificial, affected and stylised elements which Stanley scorns as 'phoney', and Williams gives her symbolic songs to sing. Stanley's language is direct, aggressive, colloquial, sometimes crude and often downright funny. Stella's language is characteristically straightforward, prosaic, sensible and down-to-earth, while Mitch's dialogue is an oddly touching mixture of the naïvely and comically simplistic and the lyrically tender.

Build critical skills

Look closely at these examples of dialogue from each of the four main characters. Analyse the ways in which Williams has given them all highly idiosyncratic speech styles to represent key aspects of their personalities.

Blanche: *He was a boy, just a boy, when I was a very young girl. When I was sixteen, I made the discovery – love. All at once and much, much too completely. It was like you suddenly turned a blinding light on something that had always been half in shadow, that's how it struck the world for me.* (page 56)

Stanley: *Don't ever talk that way to me! 'Pig – Polack – disgusting – vulgar – greasy!' – them kind of words have been on your tongue and your sister's too much around here! What do you two think you are? A pair of queens? Remember what Huey Long said – "Every Man is a King!" And I am the king around here, so don't forget it!* (page 65)

Stella: *I don't believe all of those stories and I think your supply-man was mean and rotten to tell them. It's possible that some of the things he said are partly true. There are things about my sister I don't approve of – things that caused sorrow at home. She was always – flighty!* (page 61)

Mitch: *I don't mind you being older than what I thought. But all the rest of it – God! That pitch about your ideals being so old-fashioned and all the malarkey that you've dished out all summer. Oh, I knew you weren't sixteen any more. But I was a fool enough to believe you was straight.* (page 73)

Find other examples of the dialogue given to the four main characters that you find particularly effective and analyse the ways in which Williams gives Blanche, Stanley, Stella and Mitch a distinctive speech style or idiolect. How do the ways the characters speak enhance your understanding of Williams' characterisation and themes?

Taking it further ▶

A classic episode of *The Simpsons*, 'A Streetcar Named Marge' (excerpts are on YouTube), contains humour deriving from Stanley's dialogue. This may suggest that *Streetcar* has gained that iconic status of a text that is alluded to and adapted so commonly that references simply do not require explaining.

Which aspects of Williams' form, structure, language and themes stand out to you as distinctive enough to be spoofed on a mainstream television comedy series?

Contexts

Target your learning

- What different critical positions might be applied to *A Streetcar Named Desire* to extend your knowledge of the text? (**AO1**)
- How can setting *A Streetcar Named Desire* within a broad range of contexts deepen your understanding of the play and the ways in which different audiences might respond to it? (**AO3**)
- What links might be traced between *A Streetcar Named Desire* and various other literary texts? (**AO4**)
- How can applying various critical approaches enrich your understanding of *A Streetcar Named Desire* and the ways in which different readers might interpret it? (**AO5**)

This section is designed to offer you an insight into the influence of some significant contexts in which *A Streetcar Named Desire* was written and has been performed and received, but contextual material must always be used with caution. Referencing a context is only valuable when it genuinely informs a reading of the text. Contextual material which is clumsily 'bolted on' will contribute little to your argument.

◀ A young Tennessee Williams

Biographical context

Thomas Lanier Williams was born in Mississippi in 1911, to a particularly ill-matched couple. Hard-drinking travelling salesman Cornelius Coffin Williams (C.C.) had little in common with his highly strung, snobbish wife Edwina, the daughter of a clergyman, and they were at odds for most of their married life. The middle child of three, 'Tom' was extremely close to his mother and his sister, Rose, and remained on friendly terms with his younger brother, Dakin, who was C.C.'s favourite, but he feared and hated his abusive, bullying father. This unhappy and dysfunctional family moved around a lot during his childhood and he was restless and unsettled throughout his adult life.

Context

Of Rose's decline into madness Williams (2006) wrote: 'We have had no deaths in our family but slowly by degrees something was happening much uglier and more terrible than death.' This comment - reminiscent of the Gothic horrors Blanche witnessed at Belle Reve - suggests that for Williams, who had once thought of ending *Streetcar* with his heroine throwing herself under a train, her removal to the county asylum may have been even worse.

Williams grew into a shy, gentle, artistic young man. After some early success in publishing short stories and articles he studied journalism at the University of Missouri where he was nicknamed 'Tennessee' by his fellow students on account of his Southern birth. Unfortunately C.C. forced him to withdraw from his course and get a job as a clerk at the shoe factory where he himself worked, and after three years of this drudgery, Williams had a nervous breakdown. Meanwhile his beloved sister was showing signs of severe mental illness and was diagnosed with dementia praecox (an early name for schizophrenia) at the age of just 18. Rose was subjected to an extreme and radical form of primitive brain surgery (a pre-frontal lobotomy) and then consigned to a mental institution until her death in 1996. Margaret Bradham Thornton suggests that 'the shadow of what happened to Rose stayed with [him]; she would be the model for more than fifteen characters, and Williams would give her name to many others' (Williams, 2006).

Although traumatised with guilt at what he saw as his failure to protect Rose, after transferring to the University of Iowa Williams finally graduated in 1938 at the age of 27. For the next few years he lived a bohemian and peripatetic existence while continuing to work on his short stories and plays. Finally, in 1944, *The Glass Menagerie* opened to rave reviews and made him an overnight theatrical sensation, followed three years later by the play for which he will always be remembered, the multi-award-winning *A Streetcar Named Desire*.

In the decade or so after *Streetcar*, Williams maintained a tremendous work rate, writing other major plays such as *The Rose Tattoo* (1951), *Cat on a Hot Tin Roof* (1955) and *Sweet Bird of Youth* (1959). Unfortunately, as Margaret Bradham Thornton puts it, '[this] prodigious output took its toll on Williams, and while his plays were winning awards and being made into films . . . Williams was losing his way' (Williams, 2006). Despite his professional success, his private life was always at least bordering on the chaotic and disastrous. He had a long relationship with his secretary Frank Merlo (who loyally supported Williams through frequent bouts of clinical depression) when homosexuality was still considered immoral and shocking by mainstream society, but following Merlo's death in 1963, his life seemed to spiral out of control.

Between 1959 and 1979, although he wrote 15 new plays as well as poetry, a novel and some short stories, only one work, *The Night of the Iguana* (1961) was well received, and his critical reputation went into a sharp decline which lasted until his death. At the same time his depression worsened and in 1969 his brother Dakin had to have him temporarily committed to a psychiatric hospital due to his alcoholism and drug addiction. By the time of his lonely death in a New York hotel room in 1983, the glory days were long behind him.

In his fascinating essay 'Person-to-Person', Williams wrote:

> *I still find it somehow easier to 'level with' crowds of strangers in the hushed twilight of orchestra and balcony sections of theatres than with individuals across a table from me. Their being strangers somehow makes them more familiar and more approachable, easier to talk to.*
> Williams, *Cat on a Hot Tin Roof and Other Plays*, 1976

Given this statement, although we must be careful not to assume that any text is a simplistic reworking of the writer's own personal experience, it is at least worth discussing how far his greatest and most unforgettable characters – Blanche and Stanley in *Streetcar*, Brick, Big Daddy and Maggie in *Cat on a Hot Tin Roof* and Amanda, Tom and Laura in *The Glass Menagerie*, for instance – may be seen to reflect aspects of his mother, father, sister and even himself. For many of his audiences, readers and critics, it is endlessly fascinating to speculate about the interplay between Williams' life and art, with homosexuality, mental illness, alcoholism, drug addiction, domestic violence and family dysfunction forming so large a part of his personal truth as well as his fictional world.

Historical, social and cultural contexts

The American Century and American Dream

It was Henry Luce, the influential publisher of *Life* magazine, who coined the phrase 'the American Century' to encapsulate what many people saw as the USA's duty to use its unparalleled power and influence for the greater good of the world. Writing in 1941, Luce urged his fellow Americans to enter World

Taking it further ▶

The poet Ted Hughes (1930–98) declared: 'Every work of art stems from a wound in the soul of the artist . . . Art is a psychological component of the auto-immune system that gives expression to the healing process. That is why great works of art make us feel good.' Think about the extent to which this might be true of Williams' work.

War II and back the Allies rather than remain isolated, as they had done for most of World War I. He argued:

> Throughout the 17th century and the 18th century and the 19th century, this continent teemed with manifold projects and magnificent purposes. Above them all and weaving them all together into the most exciting flag of all the world and of all history was the triumphal purpose of freedom. It is in this spirit that all of us are called, each to his own measure of capacity, and each in the widest horizon of his vision, to create the first great American Century.

This idealistic global aspiration can be seen as allied with another equally powerful myth which played out in a more domestic context: the notion of 'the American Dream'. This concept grew out of the Declaration of Independence (4 July 1776) in which the Founding Fathers of America set out their vision in the justification for breaking away from British rule:

> We hold these Truths to be self-evident that all men are created equal, that they are endowed, by their Creator, with certain unalienable Rights, that among these are Life, Liberty and the Pursuit of Happiness.

James Truslow Adams, who coined the phrase in 1931, suggested:

> [The American Dream] that has lured tens of millions of all nations to our shores in the past century has not been a dream of material plenty, though that has doubtlessly counted heavily. It has been a dream of being able to grow to fullest development as a man and woman, unhampered by the barriers which had slowly been erected in the older civilizations, unrepressed by social orders which had developed for the benefit of classes rather than for the simple human being of any and every class.

America has often portrayed itself as a 'melting pot' nation which welcomes immigrants of all races and religions to a new life of freedom and opportunity. Often escaping from poverty, oppression and conflict, America seemed a blank slate upon which they could create their vision of a land of freedom and opportunity where success depended not on birth or privilege but on hard work and courage. This idealistic vision is encapsulated in the words of Emma Lazarus (1849–87), inscribed on the pedestal of the Statue of Liberty, in which the New World of America addresses the old:

> Give me your tired, your poor,
> Your huddled masses yearning to breathe free
> The wretched refuse of your teeming shore.
> Send these, the homeless, tempest-tossed to me,
> I lift my lamp beside the golden door!

In summary, then, 'the American Century' and 'the American Dream' were concepts fully rooted in the cultural landscape of the post-war era. The former represented the USA as a kind of Good Samaritan helping other countries to achieve democracy, progress and economic security, while the latter was a way of uniting the various different groups of immigrants who came to the USA in the nineteenth and early twentieth centuries to create a cohesive national ethos.

In time, however, as things began to seem rather less glorious and more materialistic, many writers became preoccupied with showing how the American Dream had died – or even that it had only ever been an illusion in the first place. Once 'life, liberty and the pursuit of happiness' can be used to justify the actions of people – like Stanley Kowalski – who are set on claiming their slice of the action at any price, it seemed to many writers high time to question whether this mythic totem of popular culture did little more than make people increasingly unhappy, competitive and insecure. In suggesting that society was basically a level playing field, the responsibility for personal success or failure fell squarely upon the individual, and in a supposed meritocracy it can be much harder to blame one's lack of success on other people.

Thus it is in their relentless and painful probing of the gap between the underpinning cultural tradition of twentieth-century America and what they saw as the essential truth of the matter that the great tragic dramatists Tennessee Williams, Arthur Miller and Eugene O'Neill found their essential theme; they set out to question the cultural values which the vast majority of their contemporaries held dear.

The American South and New Orleans

The 'American South' is used more as an expression of an entire way of life than as a geographical location. Even today, the South has its own distinctive way of life, and its culture, food, literature and music have influenced the rest of the country immensely. Always a cultural melting pot, the South's rich mix of Native Americans, European settlers and imported African slaves has had a major impact upon its history and collective psyche.

During the American Civil War (1861–65), the Southern 'Confederate' states (including Mississippi, Alabama, Georgia, Louisiana, Texas, Virginia and Tennessee) fought against the mainly Northern 'Union' states to defend their right to keep slaves. After the heavy defeat of the South, slavery was officially abolished throughout America in 1865 and from then on the industrialised North grew inexorably more powerful, both politically and economically, than the still largely agricultural South.

Taking it further ▶

Other archetypal American Dream texts which you might enjoy comparing with *Streetcar* include F. Scott Fitzgerald's *The Great Gatsby* (1925), John Steinbeck's *Of Mice and Men* (1937), and Miller's plays *All My Sons (1947)* and *Death of a Salesman* (1949).

Context

Abraham Lincoln (1809-65) became president of the USA in 1861. Knowing that his Republican Party was anti-slavery, the Southern slave-owning states broke away from the Union. Lincoln steered his country through the Civil War, but six days after the South's final surrender he was assassinated by the fanatical Southern actor John Wilkes Booth.

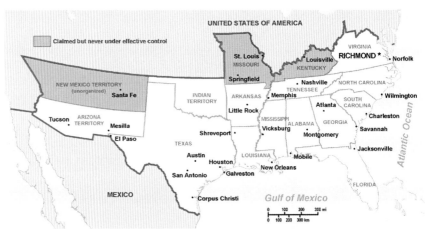

▲ The Southern states fought as the Confederate States of America in the Civil War

ante-bellum: (from Latin meaning 'before the war') often used of the Old South prior to the defining event of the American Civil War.

After the Civil War, many white southerners bought into an enduring nostalgic mythic representation of the South in its ***ante-bellum*** heyday as a haven of peace, prosperity and chivalrous gallantry. For black southerners the Old South was a completely different story. In *Streetcar*, which is set more than 80 years after the end of the Civil War, it is still possible to see that the seeds of the events that lead to Blanche's tragic downfall were sown way back in time when the degenerate aristocratic DuBois began to drink, whore and gamble away Belle Reve, which we can be sure was anything but a beautiful dream for the slaves who worked the plantation.

New Orleans, the city in which Blanche found herself a stranger, is world famous for its multicultural and multilingual heritage and as the birthplace of jazz. However, all the beautiful Spanish-style architecture, dazzling Mardi Gras parades and delicious soul food cannot obscure the extreme poverty in which many of its inhabitants live even today. In some people's eyes, 'the Big Easy' should never have been built where it was; the climate is hot and humid, and because it is surrounded by water on three sides, flooding is a constant risk.

Context

After Hurricane Katrina (2005), when 80 per cent of the city's 225,000 inhabitants had to be evacuated when the city flooded, there was a feeling that the federal government would have acted more decisively if rich white northerners had been affected rather than poor, mainly black southerners.

In *Streetcar*, Williams dramatises a brutal culture clash between the New Orleans industrial worker and his aristocratic intellectual rival. Enraged and intimidated by the old-fashioned Southern values Blanche embodies, Stanley determines – albeit unconsciously at first – to destroy the threat she poses to his brave new world. Stella is presented as caught between her loyalty to the 'beautiful dream' of the past, symbolised by Blanche and their lost childhood home in the countryside, and the brash and thrilling immediacy of her new life in the big city of New Orleans. Once upon a time Blanche might have defined herself solely in terms of her status as a ladylike southerner and even after her arrival in New Orleans' Vieux Carré she persists in keeping up this act because it is so much less painful than facing the truth about her penniless, hard-drinking, promiscuous existence. But Stanley – go-getting, practical, down-to-earth and materialistic – will have none of it. Stella's baby is born on the very night he brutally rapes Blanche and tips her into outright madness; Stella's decision to stay with the father of her child and allow her sister to be committed to a mental asylum may symbolise the shifting social power structures of the new America.

Smith-Howard and Heintzelman (2005) have noted the significance of the clash between Blanche and Stanley over the loss of Belle Reve in Scene II; what the plantation represents to each of them is powerfully suggestive. Belle Reve:

> is Blanche's lost, beautiful dream, rich with family heritage and pride; Stanley is interested only in the property's material or monetary real estate value. He is happy in the loud, harsh, and dirty world of the Vieux Carré of New Orleans, whereas Blanche prefers finer accommodations, the bucolic setting of hundreds of acres of land and large white pillars on a grand veranda that provide lounging quarters out of the midday sun.

Ironically the Belle Reve Blanche lost was in fact a very twisted version of this 'lost beautiful dream'; a Gothic horror straight out of the nightmare stories of Poe.

Stanley is a second-generation immigrant industrial worker who lives in Elysian Fields (an appropriate setting for a war hero) but here Blanche's genteel values are totally out of context. Thus as emblems of the moribund Southern aristocracy on the one hand and an energetic immigrant community determined to make its way in the world on the other, Blanche and Stanley are engaged in a desperate struggle only one of them can win; Stanley declares just before he rapes her, **'We've had this date with each other from the beginning!'**. It is certainly possible to see Blanche as a lost soul trapped in limbo between the old world and the new; as Williams' great contemporary Elia Kazan put it, she is 'a last dying relic . . . now adrift in our unfriendly day'.

> Top ten quotation

Build critical skills

The poet and critic T.S. Eliot coined the term 'objective correlative' to describe the way in which objects, situations or events are used to represent characters or emotions. How far do you think it is true to say that Belle Reve is the objective correlative for Blanche's identity as a Southern belle?

Context

G.P.A. Healy's famous portrait *The Southern Belle* (1860) shows the beautiful Miss Sallie Ward of Louisville, Kentucky, in her prime. You can view the painting online.

▲ The Vieux Carre district of New Orleans

Gender roles

During World War II women had become used to filling the men's roles in the workplace and had gained considerable freedom and financial independence; for a while it had seemed possible for women to pursue their own version of the American Dream. *A Streetcar Named Desire* presents a sharp critique of the way the institutions and attitudes of post-war America affected women's lives, just as later, in *Cat on a Hot Tin Roof*, the rivalry between Maggie and Mae raises questions about the role of college-educated women in the 1950s and the extent to which they were still defined by their fertility and domesticity. Many of Williams' female characters seem psychologically trapped in the cultural pragmatics of the Old South, as Blanche and Stella's dependence on men exposes attitudes to women during the transition from the old world to the new. Both Blanche and Stella – and Eunice, for that matter – see male companions as their only means to achieve happiness and depend on men for both economic and psychological reasons. When Stanley uses the Napoleonic code to try to muscle in on Stella's inheritance it seems exploitative, yet Blanche's escape plan (throwing herself on the mercy of Shep Huntleigh) still involves playing a submissive and dependent role. Ironically, when Blanche invokes the vision of Shep arriving to rescue her in Scene XI, it is in fact the doctor who offers her his gentlemanlike support when he escorts her to the asylum.

Literary context

Intertextuality

The influential French feminist and literary theorist Julia Kristeva (b. 1941) coined the term 'intertextuality' in 1966 to describe the complex network of links which exist between texts. Working with Kristeva's notion of intertextuality allows us to place *Streetcar* at the centre of a web of interconnected texts and contexts that show just how fascinating and challenging the play remains, almost 70 years after it was written.

Southern Gothic

Feminist critic Molly Haskell, herself a southerner, has described:

> [T]he attraction of the Lost Cause mythology – we were grander, purer in defeat than were those crass, winner-take-all Yankees with their greedy industrial culture. The myth of the Lost Cause and the moral superiority of losing defined and fed our romantic sense of ourselves, our specialness, our region marked by a defeat that wasn't quite a defeat in a war that wasn't quite over.
>
> M. Haskell, *Frankly, My Dear: 'Gone with the Wind' Revisited*, 2009

As a writer closely associated with the Southern Gothic genre, Williams overhauls and deconstructs the traditional stereotype of the demure Southern belle by making Blanche DuBois not just the damsel in distress she pretends to

CRITICAL VIEW

Kristeva, like Roland Barthes, sees 'meaning' not as an intrinsic part of a text but as brought to it by individual readers. Through 'intertextuality', meaning is mediated through the writer's and reader's awareness of other texts. Make a list of all the literary texts Williams refers to within the text and try to analyse why he has chosen them.

be for her naïve suitor Mitch's benefit, but also a promiscuous alcoholic who threatens to trash her sister's marriage.

Williams once described Southern Gothic as allied with 'an underlying dreadfulness in modern experience' and his adoption of the nickname 'Tennessee' was an acknowledgement of his conscious commitment to dramatising the culture, values and conflicts of his native land. In 'Person-to-Person', Williams captured the tragicomic desperation of the Southern experience in general and the Southern writer in particular in this memorable vignette:

> *I once saw a group of little girls on a Mississippi sidewalk, all dolled up in their mothers' and sisters' cast-off finery, old raggedy ball gowns and plumed hats and high-heeled slippers, enacting a meeting of ladies in a parlour with a perfect mimicry of Southern gush and simper. But one child was not satisfied with the attention paid her performance by the others ... so she stretched out her skinny arms and threw back her skinny neck and shrieked to the deaf heavens and her equally oblivious playmates, 'Look at me, look at me, look at me!'*
>
> *And then her mother's high-heeled slippers threw her off balance and she fell to the sidewalk in a great howling tangle of soiled white satin and torn pink net, and still nobody looked at her.*
>
> *I wonder if she is not, now, a Southern writer.*

Williams, Cat on a Hot Tin Roof, 1976

Williams' contemporary Flannery O'Connor, one little girl who did grow up to be a Southern writer, noted with irony the cultural divide between the North and the South:

> *[A]nything that comes out of the South is going to be called grotesque by the northern reader, unless it is grotesque, in which case it is going to be called realistic.*

Like O'Connor and many other practitioners working within the Southern Gothic genre, Williams dramatises with both humour and pathos the apparent inability of the genteel gracious gallantry of the mythic antique Old South to survive amid the brash consumerist confidence of booming post-war America, and never more powerfully than in *Streetcar*, in which this debate is framed around the binary oppositions embodied by Stanley and Blanche, the future and the past.

Finally, when the doctor arrives at the end of *Streetcar* to escort Blanche to the lunatic asylum, he ironically conforms to the heroine's outdated notion of the chivalrous Southern beau who will offer her the gentlemanly support and kindness she craves so desperately. Her ultimate collapse can be seen as the apocalyptic meltdown of an entire semi-mythological culture.

The epigraph: Hart Crane

And so it was I entered the broken world

To trace the visionary company of love, its voice

An instant in the wind (I know not whither hurled)

But not for long to hold each desperate choice.

The epigraph to *A Streetcar Named Desire* is the fifth stanza of Hart Crane's poem 'The Broken Tower'. Williams admired and identified with Crane (1899–1932) and there are significant parallels between their lives; both had difficult relationships with their parents, struggled with alcoholism and were trying to find their identities as gay men at a time when there was still intense social and cultural stigma attached to homosexuality. Like the tortured young poet Allan Grey in *Streetcar*, Hart Crane committed suicide at a tragically young age; because 'The Broken Tower' was the last poem he wrote before his death, some readers have seen it as akin to his last will and testament. As Gilbert Debusscher has noted, '[a]mong the few permanent possessions Williams took with him on his constant peregrinations were a copy of Hart Crane's collected poems and a framed portrait of the poet' (Debusscher in Roudané, 1997). Williams made sure that the epigraph was printed in the theatre programmes to make it as easy for an audience to compare Crane's words with his drama as for a reader; the poem captures a sense of love as a transitory illusion or gambler's 'desperate choice', which is strongly suggestive of Blanche's experience of love in a 'broken world'.

Build critical skills

One very well-known example of the Southern Gothic genre is Harper Lee's novel *To Kill a Mockingbird* (1960). The text features an elderly neighbour addicted to morphine, a rabid dog wandering the streets, a bizarre fire that destroys another neighbour's house, the feral Ewell family, the local superstitions about Boo Radley and the attack on the Finch children in the dark woods. Review the elements in *Streetcar* that might place it within the Southern Gothic framework.

Romanticism

Romanticism (c. 1770–1830) was a European cultural phenomenon which encompassed not only literature in all its forms but also art, music, politics, philosophy, science and religion. Set against a historical background of radical change in which traditional social, religious, economic and political beliefs were challenged and reinterpreted, it followed on from and partly rebelled against the previous age of Enlightenment, preferring originality, imagination and freedom to reason, self-restraint and order.

Taking it further

You can read the full text of 'The Broken Tower' online. Go to http://oldpoetry.com and search on 'Harold Hart Crane'; click on 'The Broken Tower'.

Taking it further

It is interesting to compare Williams' dramatic representations of the South (and its women) with the work of some female prose writers associated with the Southern Gothic genre. You might begin by dipping into Carson McCullers' *The Ballad of the Sad Cafe* (1951), Flannery O'Connor's *Everything That Rises Must Converge* (1965) or Donna Tartt's *The Little Friend* (2002).

The word Romantic is linked to the French word *romance* and implies a search for meaning and identity. The Romantics believed that artists should seek the essential truth about life and mediate that truth through their own personal experiences. Their quintessential archetype was the Byronic hero, an anti-Establishment outcast who hovered on the margins of mainstream society, questioning its values, conventions and ideas. The origin of this archetype was the poet Lord Byron himself, a legendary figure whose significance as a cultural icon proved hugely influential both during his own lifetime and for generations to come. Above all, Byron's wandering exile has come to symbolise the Romantic quest for freedom, mobility and space in a harsh and unsympathetic world.

In many ways Williams himself was just such an artistic and cultural outsider, 'a poet in a practical world, a homosexual in a heterosexual society', as Nancy M. Tischler has written (Tischler in Roudané, 1997). Williams, like Byron, Poe and Crane, was a misfit whose imagination and poetic spirit left him out of tune with the pragmatic mores of his contemporary society. He regretted the loss of the South's traditional creed of elegance, beauty and gallantry and his plays are scattered with romantic dreamers like Blanche – and himself – tragically out of place in the new America and driven to use sex, alcohol and often drugs as a means of escape. The interweaving of his lush, sometimes grandiose romantic visions and the grimy reality of ordinary life is one of the hallmarks of Williams' life and work, and in *Streetcar* the clash between Romanticism and pragmatism is encapsulated by the opposing figures of Blanche and Stanley.

CRITICAL VIEW

The director Elia Kazan, who worked with Williams often, said: 'everything in his life is in his plays, and everything in his plays is in his life'. Williams himself said: 'I can't expose a human weakness on the stage unless I know it through having it myself'. How far do you find this psychological interpretation a useful critical lens to apply to the play?

Context

The public image of Lord Byron (1788-1824) played as great a role in his success as did his poetry. Lionised by literary London, he was run out of town when rumours spread about his unorthodox love life; he had an affair with his half-sister and was sexually attracted to young boys. By 1816 he was living a nomadic life abroad, in permanent exile from England. He died in Greece at the age of 36.

Parallels with *Cat on a Hot Tin Roof*

Cat on a Hot Tin Roof (1955) also dramatises Williams' ideas of history, family, religion and community and minutely deconstructs traditional Southern stereotypes as Williams entwines the tragic stories of a powerful man who wrongly thinks he has cheated death and his once famous and idolised son. Both Big Daddy Pollitt and his younger son Brick can be viewed through the dramatic prism of classical and Shakespearian tragedy, as both characters are highly gifted but also deeply flawed. Brick's weary lethargy is reminiscent of Hamlet's inability to act decisively and face up to a family crisis, and perhaps even more resonant is Williams' decision to have the fallen sporting idol hobble about with his broken foot in a cast, given that the name 'Oedipus', the most famous of all tragic heroes, may be translated literally as 'swollen foot'.

This book has already mentioned several comparisons and connections between *Streetcar* and *Cat on a Hot Tin Roof*, but there are others:

- Like Blanche, Maggie can be seen as the archetypal demure Southern belle pining for a chivalrous beau viewed through a distorted lens. While many of the minor characters in *Streetcar* provide evidence of the easy, bustling multicultural nature of working-class New Orleans, in *Cat on a Hot Tin Roof* the comfortable caricature of the happy slave or 'Uncle Tom' is undermined by Williams' symbolic use of the Pollitt's black servants, never seen but heard off stage at key dramatic moments. When Mae cries, 'Oh Big Daddy, the field hands are singing for you!' the servants' chosen spiritual is 'Pick a bale of cotton', a song about the hardships of slavery which reminds the audience that the Pollitt inheritance was founded on the forced labour of thousands of black agricultural workers.

- Both texts deal with families and inheritance; up for grabs in *Cat on a Hot Tin Roof* is Big Daddy's $10 million fortune, '28,000 acres of the richest land this side of the valley Nile', and the family vultures are circling even before he realises he's dying. In *Streetcar*, although Belle Reve was lost before the action of the play begins, Stanley hopes, (like Mae and Gooper in *Cat*) that legal documents will prove his claim.

- Both Blanche and Brick prefer to live in the past, before the suicide of the homosexual characters they loved and lost. They are haunted by guilt at having responded harshly to Allan and Skipper respectively. (Like Allan, Skipper never appears on stage.)

- Brick and Blanche both use alcohol to numb their emotional pain and retreat to the bathroom in times of stress.

- Both Big Daddy's and Blanche's birthday parties end disastrously.

- Both plays metaphorically link desire and death, in that while Blanche's streetcar is heading for Cemeteries, in *Cat on a Hot Tin Roof* it's a toss-up as to whether Mae's sixth baby will arrive before Big Daddy dies of cancer – 'the stork and the reaper are running neck-and-neck'.

- The plays end with the real or imagined birth of a baby: Stella and Stanley's son and a projected one 'sired by Brick, and out of Maggie the Cat!'

- Blanche and Brick clash violently with Stanley and Big Daddy; in each case romantic ruin is offset with brute strength and vigorous vulgarity.

- The cheap collapsible camp-bed upon which Stanley rapes Blanche is paralleled by the huge double bed which dominates Brick and Maggie's bedroom in *Cat on a Hot Tin Roof*. This is the marital bed in which the glamorous young couple no longer make love; as Big Mama says, pointing at the bed, 'When a marriage goes on the rocks, the rocks are *there*, right *there*!'

▲ Vivien Leigh as Scarlett O'Hara on the family's plantation Tara in the film *Gone with the Wind* (1939)

Performance context

The 1951 Kazan film: Vivien Leigh and Marlon Brando

Vivien Leigh was a Hollywood celebrity who had won an Academy Award for her iconic performance as the wilful and beautiful Southern belle Scarlett O'Hara in *Gone with the Wind* (1939). Adapted from Margaret Mitchell's 1936 novel, *Gone with the Wind* is still probably the most famous film ever made and certainly the high-water mark of Hollywood's golden age. Leigh was a little-known English actress when she won the part of Scarlett in a blaze of publicity following a three-year search for the perfect heroine; if not quite the rags-to-riches cliché of the understudy who becomes an overnight star, it was as close as made no difference.

The beautiful, flirtatious and yet innocent belle was the quintessential pattern of ideal young womanhood among the aristocracy of the doomed Old South, and in *Gone With The Wind* Scarlett O'Hara's story plays out against the epic backdrop of the American Civil War. As Molly Haskell suggests, Scarlett is a fascinating character:

> [P]oised at one of those pivotal moments in the redefining of women's roles ... when the entire catechism of traditional womanly virtues – piety, chastity, sacrifice, living through and for others, and unflagging loyalty to family and country – virtues held up since time immemorial, seem to be turned on their head! In their place are offered such alarmingly worldly aspirations as self-fulfilment, sexual freedom, mobility, choice, and appetite for things beyond home and family.
>
> Haskell, 2009

It is worth bearing in mind that *Gone with the Wind*'s most famous location, Tara, the fabled plantation which Scarlett adores, would have been the iconic template evoked in the minds of most of Williams' contemporaries with every mention of Belle Reve in *A Streetcar Named Desire*. While Blanche is far more fragile than the feisty Scarlett, as John Russell Taylor has noted:

> [S]he does set one wondering what happened to that kind of Southern belle with the passage of time and the decay of the South, and

Scarlett's obsession with Tara is well matched by Blanche's with Belle Reve. More specifically, what would have become of Scarlett when she had aged and her beauty faded to a degree that she could not always get her own way just by stamping her little foot?

J.R. Taylor, *Vivien Leigh*, 1984

Context

'People have speculated that Williams had Leigh in mind when he wrote *Streetcar* and created the other great Southern belle of the twentieth century', notes Molly Haskell in *Frankly, My Dear: 'Gone with the Wind' Revisited* (2009): '... there's a lot of Scarlett in Blanche, the Southern beauty cast back on her own fragile resources ... [yet] the clear-eyed Scarlett ... unlike Blanche, sees things as they are and never looks back, never yields either to nostalgia or to the temptation of vice'.

Legend has it that while Leigh was not director Elia Kazan's first choice to play Blanche in the 1951 film version of *A Streetcar Named Desire*, he was intrigued by the idea of watching Scarlett O'Hara go mad. Jessica Tandy, who played Blanche in the original Broadway stage production, was in any case not a big enough box-office star to headline an edgy production which dealt with rape, promiscuity and homosexuality. Given that Leigh's role as Scarlett meant that for a whole generation of cinema-goers she simply *was* the archetypal belle of American popular culture, her wrecked and ruined turn as Williams' belle gone bad seems to capture something of the apparently inevitable decline of the South itself.

Whereas Leigh was Hollywood royalty, the casting of Marlon Brando as Stanley offers a sense of life shadowing art. At first mocked by traditionalists for his 'mumbling' delivery, he was instantly acclaimed by the younger generation as a ground-breaking new acting talent; according to film director Martin Scorsese, he was 'the marker': 'There's "before Brando" and "after Brando."' Unlike the classically trained Leigh, Marlon Brando was closely associated with the modern 'Method' school of acting. Working with the ideas of the Russian actor and director Konstantin Stanislavski, 'Method' actors sought to tap into the psychology of their characters in order to inhabit them more fully.

In some ways the fundamental contrast between Brando and Leigh as practitioners of their craft echoes the unbridgeable gulf between Stanley and Blanche, yet to the surprise of many, in the words of the film critic Pauline Kael, this chalk-and-cheese combination gave 'two of the greatest performances ever put on film', with Leigh's Blanche 'one of those rare performances that can truly be said to evoke both fear and pity'. Leigh herself, who suffered from periodic bouts of manic depression and mental illness, admitted, 'I had nine months in the theatre of Blanche DuBois. Now she's in command of me.' Indeed, while Williams felt Leigh's Blanche was 'everything that I intended, and much that I had never dreamed of', the actress herself felt that playing the role had 'tipped me over into madness'.

Given that the roles with which Leigh is indelibly associated reflect the same mythic cultural archetype of the Southern belle, it seems fitting that at the 1951 Academy Awards she was named Best Actress for playing Blanche DuBois just as she had been for Scarlett O'Hara 12 years before. Karl Malden and Kim Hunter also won Oscars as Best Supporting Actor and Actress for their portrayals of Mitch and Stella, but the Academy failed to acknowledge Marlon Brando's electrifying portrayal of Stanley despite its having established him as perhaps the greatest film actor of the post-war era. Even in later years, when his fatal cocktail of hubristic arrogance and self-indulgence had virtually destroyed his career, his rare screen appearances were still greeted as major cultural events. Appropriately enough, his most famous screen performance was as another working-class outsider determined to find his own inverted version of the American Dream – Vito Corleone, the penniless Sicilian immigrant who becomes a Mafia don in Francis Ford Coppola's *The Godfather* (1972).

Changes from stage to screen

Several of the changes from stage to screen made in the 1951 Kazan film suggest that what was acceptable to an elite, sophisticated, minority Broadway theatre audience was unacceptable in a mainstream, conservative Hollywood film production context. Bound as it was by the notoriously restrictive film Production Code, as R. Barton Palmer notes, Hollywood 'was committed to banishing from significant representation or often mere mention the themes Williams found so compelling and unavoidable'. In effect, the Code dictated that films had to 'be structured by the central principle of nineteenth-century melodrama: evil was to be punished and good rewarded, while any sympathy for wrongdoing should be eliminated by compensating moral value (such as the unlikely reform in the last five minutes of hitherto enthusiastic sinners)'.

Streetcar's exploration of many areas of human existence which the Code defined as off-limits – alcoholism, promiscuity, rape, homosexuality and madness – was problematic enough, while the fact that Stanley's rape of his sister-in-law goes officially unpunished created a particular dilemma, even if Blanche's own sexual transgressions meant that 'suffering for a less-than-virtuous female main character did not violate then-acceptable notions of a poetically just ending' (Barton Palmer in Roudané, 1997).

At this point, it is worth setting *Streetcar* against the highly specific cultural context of the signature movie genre of the 1940s, the *film noir* (from the French for 'black cinema'). The leading female characters of these sexy, stylish crime melodramas were often treacherous *femmes fatales* who broke the rules of mainstream society and were brutally punished for their actions, while their male counterparts were often cynical private detectives bent on ferreting out their guilty secrets; there are obvious ironic parallels here with the roles of Blanche and Stanley. As Barton Palmer has noted, since the *film noir* genre popular at the time frequently featured attractive but morally ambiguous *femmes fatales* who wound up 'dead, imprisoned, or otherwise punished', *Streetcar*'s shocking conclusion 'would be acceptable to filmgoers used to similar portrayals of feminine misadventure'.

After the film was completed, however, the censors demanded certain cuts and alterations which were made without the consent of either Williams or director Elia Kazan, as Smith-Howard and Heintzelman (2005) note.

The major cuts were:

- several close-up shots which overtly emphasised the sexual passion between Stanley and Stella
- the rape scene, leaving Stanley's attack implied rather than obvious
- several references to Blanche's promiscuous past.

The major alteration was to the ending of the play. The censors did not wish to have Stanley appear to 'get away with' his near-incestuous rape, so the famous final 'Holy Family' tableau of Stella, Stanley and the baby was removed. Instead, Stella rebels against Stanley, seizing the baby and telling him: 'We're never going back. Never, never back. Never back again.' The film closes with her running upstairs to Eunice, as she did at the end of the poker night, while once again Stanley bellows: 'STELL-LAHHHHHH!'

Taking it further ▶

Watch a classic film noir such as *Laura* (1944), *Double Indemnity* (1945) or *The Postman Always Rings Twice* (1946) and compare the sexual tension that exists between the male and female leads with Williams' portrayal of Blanche and Stanley in *A Streetcar Named Desire*. You can find out more about the *noir* genre online at www.filmnoirstudies.com.

Build critical skills

AO5 requires you to demonstrate an understanding that the meaning of a text is not 'fixed' and that at various places within a text different interpretations are possible. These different interpretations may be supported by reference to the ideas of named critics or particular critical perspectives, but may also emerge from your own discussions with other students and your teacher. What matters is that you have come to a personal interpretation of the play through an understanding of a variety of ways of making meanings.

TASK

Watch the final scene of the 1951 film version two or three times and compare it closely to the printed text. Given its very close parallels with the end of Scene III (the Poker Night), how likely is it, in your opinion, that Stella really will leave Stanley this time, as the film suggests?

CRITICAL VIEW

As well as Roland Barthes, other critics closely associated with reader-response include the German Wolfgang Iser (1926–2007) and the American Stanley Fish (b. 1938). You might wish to research their ideas using the internet and see how far you think they might be applied to *Streetcar* and the other texts you are studying for A-level.

Critical approaches

Ways of thinking about texts

In 1968 the French literary theorist Roland Barthes wrote a hugely influential essay called *The Death of the Author* in which he argued that the idea of an author or authority led people to believe it was possible to decode and hence explain the essential 'meaning' of a text. For Barthes, the multiple different ways of making meaning in language, and the fact that it is impossible to know the author's state of mind, made a mockery of the idea of a 'knowable text'. The Marxist Barthes saw the concept of the author as another method of transforming a text into a consumer product which could be used up and replaced in a bourgeois, westernised capitalist culture.

While the 'death of the author' theory might at first seem to suggest that Barthes effectively cut the reader's safety rope and left him or her dangling off a literary cliff, in fact his ideas can be seen as heralding the 'birth of the reader'. The reader-response approach to literature suggests that writers and readers collaborate to make meanings and that as readers our responses will depend upon our own experiences, ideas and values. Unlike literary theories or critical positions which concentrate on the author, content or form of the text, reader-response theory privileges the role of the active reader in creating textual meanings. If you remember this, you may well feel more confident in assessing the performances, interpretations and literary-critical points of view you encounter. Moreover, by setting the play at the centre of an intertextual web of contexts and connections you can start to trace the assumptions underlying both *Streetcar* itself and the responses of various readers and audiences to the text. By resisting the notion of fixed meanings, you are free to make the most of the shifting and unstable nature of the text itself. Thus while this section covers a variety of modern critical approaches that can shed considerable light on the play, remember that you too are a critic, and as such you should always try to form your own interpretation of the text.

Feminist criticism

Feminist critics are interested in how women are represented in literature, challenging dominant traditional attitudes and ideas about how female characters (who are often seen through the eyes of male writers) feel, act and think. Feminist criticism challenges patriarchal assumptions by unpicking the gender stereotyping embodied in a text and exploring how such stereotypes can be undermined and resisted. Given that the central protagonist is a woman, it is hard to envisage studying *A Streetcar Named Desire* without applying a feminist critique of some kind, while key issues associated with traditional male and female gender roles such as childbirth, homemaking, sex and work are extensively debated within the text. Relationships between Blanche, Stella and Eunice are vividly drawn, interestingly problematic and highly convincing, while male-female relationships are analysed and dissected in forensic detail.

Nevertheless, given that the play was written 70 years ago, it is worth asking yourself if there are any aspects of the ways in which female characters are represented within it that may seem dated or stereotyped now.

▲ A woman engaged in stereotypical 1940's gender roles

Feminist criticism challenges assumptions about gender and exposes both the sexual stereotyping embodied in a text and the way in which such stereotypes might be subverted. Feminist critics attempt to describe and interpret women's experience as depicted in literature. They question long-standing dominant patriarchal attitudes, ideologies and interpretations and challenge traditional ideas about how women are (according to male writers) supposed to feel, act and think. Whether *Streetcar* exhibits feminist sympathies or merely accepts the patriarchal status quo, sexual double standard and cultural misogyny of its time is an issue that can only enhance your analysis of the roles of Blanche, Stella and even Eunice.

CRITICAL VIEW

Felicia Hardison Londré suggests that Scene IV 'strongly invites feminist criticism', since Blanche's only solution to what she sees as Stella's degraded life with Stanley is to look up her old beau Shep Huntleigh. While Blanche sees Stanley as a brutal ape, as Londré points out, 'there is a subtle irony in her reflexive reversion to the Southern belle's habits of thought – that is, emotional dependence on a patriarchal system of male protection for the helpless female – just moments after she has said, 'I'm going to do something. Get hold of myself and make myself a new life!' (Londré in Roudané, 1997). How do you respond to this view of Williams' representation of Blanche here?

Political criticism

The German philosopher and political thinker Karl Marx (1818–83) was the founder of modern communism. In *The Communist Manifesto* (1848), Marx stated: 'The history of all hitherto existing society is the history of class struggles.' Thus a Marxist literary critical perspective sees works of literature as inevitably conditioned by and reflective of the economic and political forces of their social context.

TASK

From a feminist point of view, do you see Blanche's 'emotional dependence' as just part of the play's social context, or is it in fact specific to her character? Do you think Stella can be seen as any less 'emotionally dependent' than her sister?

Political criticism might include Marxist analysis and New Historicism. It reminds us that literary texts are products of a particular set of socio-political circumstances from which they cannot be divorced, and that they are informed by a range of cultural preoccupations and anxieties that manifest themselves regardless of whether they are consciously intended by the writer or not. Marxist critics see literary texts as material products which are part of – and help to explain – the processes of history, as Terry Eagleton notes:

> Marxist criticism is not merely a 'sociology of literature', concerned with how novels get published and whether they mention the working class. Its aim is to explain the literary work more fully; and this means a sensitive attention to its forms, styles and meanings. But it also means grasping those forms, styles and meanings as the product of a particular history.

> T. Eagleton, *Marxism and Literary Criticism*, 1976

It was Williams' great contemporary Arthur Miller (1915–2005) who recognised that, although not an overtly 'political' playwright like Miller himself, Williams was still very much engaged with the warp and weft of contemporary American society. For Miller, a character like Blanche DuBois, whose waning social, political and economic authority encapsulates the uneasy tension between the legendary romantic ante-bellum South and its terrible history of slavery and oppression, is by definition clearly and heavily politicised.

According to Christopher Bigsby, however, Williams (who only voted once in his life) was if anything a 'profoundly conservative' writer. 'What he wanted above all was for the individual to be left alone, insulated from the pressure of public event', although 'even if his radicalism is better viewed as a celebration of the outcast or the deprived, a sympathy for those discarded by a society for which he anyway had little sympathy, his work reveals a consistent distrust of the wealthy and powerful, a suspicion of materialism' (Bigsby, *Modern American Drama*, 2000).

In his 1949 essay 'Tragedy and the Common Man', Miller tried to define what it was that still moved contemporary audiences when watching a classical tragedy, given that the contexts of production and reception were so far removed from each other, and that therefore we cannot care very much about 'the right of one monarch to capture the domain from another' when 'our concepts of justice [are not] what they were to the mind of an Elizabethan king'. Instead, Miller argued:

> The quality in such plays that does shake us, however, derives from the underlying fear of being displaced, the disaster inherent in being torn away from our chosen image of what or who we are in this world. Among us today this fear is as strong, and perhaps stronger, than it ever was. In fact, it is the common man who knows this fear best.

Furthermore, he added:

> [I]f it is true to say that in essence the tragic hero is intent upon claiming his whole due as a personality, and if this struggle must be

total and without reservation, then it automatically demonstrates the indestructible will of man to achieve his humanity. The possibility of victory must be there in tragedy. Where pathos rules, where pathos is finally derived, a character has fought a battle he could not possibly have won. The pathetic is achieved when the protagonist is ... incapable of grappling with a much superior force ... But tragedy requires a nicer balance between what is possible and what is impossible. And it is curious, although edifying, that the plays we revere, century after century, are the tragedies. In them, and in them alone, lies the belief – optimistic, if you will, in the perfectibility of man. It is time, I think, that we who are without kings, took up this bright thread of our history and followed it to the only place it can possibly lead in our time – the heart and spirit of the average man.

CRITICAL VIEW

Arguably the fact that Stanley and Blanche clash so ferociously over economic issues reveals the increasingly consumerist and materialistic nature of the American Dream, and a Marxist reading of *Streetcar* might suggest that human relationships are inevitably warped and distorted by the forces of a capitalist social and political system. How far do you agree with this view?

TASK

Read the full text of Miller's hugely influential short essay online at http://theliterarylink. com/miller1.html.

One very interesting outcome of trying to apply Miller's ideas to *Streetcar* is the extent to which it seems easier to fit Stanley into his 'common man' tragic paradigm than Blanche. It certainly appears true to say that both characters might be seen as sharing 'the underlying fear of being displaced, the disaster inherent in being torn away from our chosen image of what or who we are in this world' and thus 'intent upon claiming [their] whole due as a personality'. Yet beyond this, surely Blanche's struggle would be defined as pathetic rather than tragic in Miller's eyes, since she is so clearly fighting 'a battle [s]he could not possibly have won' and is 'incapable of grappling with a much superior force'. Stanley's battle, on the other hand, is 'total and without reservation' and thus 'automatically demonstrates the indestructible will of man to achieve his humanity'. Once again, it seems, the vexed debate about the identity of the hero and anti-hero – the protagonist and the antagonist – of *Streetcar* can be thrown wide open.

Psychoanalytic criticism

Sigmund Freud published one of the founding texts of psychoanalysis, *The Interpretation of Dreams*, in 1900. Psychoanalytic critics see literature as like dreams. Both are fictions, inventions of the mind that, although based on reality, are not literally true. Psychoanalytic criticism explores the significance of the subconscious as a means of exploring the representation of character. Much psychoanalytical criticism is based on the theories of Freud, and explores the effect of dreams, fantasies, unconscious desires and aspects of sexuality.

In *A Streetcar Named Desire*, aspects of the text that lend themselves to psychoanalytic readings include Blanche's flashbacks and nightmares, the linking of sex and death and the overtly sexual nature of much of the imagery of the play.

CRITICAL VIEW

Blanche hands the documents over to Stanley, saying: 'I think it's wonderfully fitting that Belle Reve should finally be this bunch of old papers in your big, capable hands!'. Later she tells Stella 'maybe he's what we need to mix with our blood now that we've lost Belle Reve'. Robert Bray interprets this as a transfer of power from the rural Old South to the industrial new America (Londré in Roudané, 1997). What do you think?

In Freudian terms, two sexual traumas – one in the past (her discovery of Allan's homosexuality) and one in the present (her rape) – destroy Blanche's fragile hold on sanity. She attempts to repress her memories of the past through taking refuge in art, music and literature – as well as lots of illicit and unauthorised sex. For most modern readers, it is hard not to read the streetcar which 'bangs through the Quarter, up one old narrow street and down another' as a graphically blunt metaphor for the sexual act itself, while the phallic symbolism of the poker game (in which 'one-eyed jacks are wild' and the game is **'seven-card stud'**, seems equally ominous. Moreover, the polarised streetcar destinations of Desire and Cemeteries certainly lend themselves to being considered in terms of Freud's belief that humans are motivated by two conflicting central desires, *eros* (which is creative, life-producing and thus drives sexual passion and love) and its opposite, *thanatos*, the death instinct, which wills us towards calm, oblivion and death.

Top ten quotation

Queer theory

The term 'queer theory' was coined in 1990, but since the late 1960s, as Julie Rivkin and Michael Ryan note, critics had begun to examine the 'history of the oppression of gays, lesbians, and practitioners of sexualities other than those deemed normal by the dominant heterosexual group', as well as the 'countercultures of gay and lesbian writing that existed in parallel fashion with the dominant heterosexual culture' (Rivkin and Ryan, Literary Theory, 1999: 888). Queer theory is grounded in a debate about whether a person's sexuality is part of their essential self or socially constructed, and queer theorists question the ways in which heterosexuality is presented as 'normal' and focus on 'non-heteronormative' sexual behaviour. Queer theory is a particularly interesting way of looking at the life and work of Williams because, as a gay man, Williams was forced to disguise his challenging ideas about licit and illicit sexuality by focalising them through a female heroine.

As Christopher Bigsby suggests, Williams' outsider status may be seen as one of the reasons he became a master of the dramatic form, a genre which, by definition, involves multiple ways of making meaning:

> *Since Williams is the poet of the unauthorised, the unsanctioned, the outlawed, it seems logical that he should choose a form which more easily releases its pluralism of meanings – under the pressure of actors, director, audience – than does the poem or the novel. It is not that novels have restrictive meanings but that the incompletions of the theatrical text are readily apparent, indeed implicit in the form.*
>
> Bigsby, 2000

Moreover, as Miller argued in his autobiography *Timebends* (1987), Williams' identity as a gay man inevitably politicised both his life and his art:

> *If only because he came up at a time when homosexuality was absolutely unacknowledged in a public figure, Williams had to belong to a minority culture and understood in his bones what a brutal menace the majority could be if aroused against him ... Certainly I never regarded him as the sealed-off aesthete he was thought to be. There is a radical politics of the soul as well as of the ballot box and the picket line. If he was not an activist it was not for the lack of a desire for justice, nor did he consider a theatre profoundly involved in society and politics ... beyond his interest.*

Build critical skills

Critics closely associated with queer theory include the American critics Eve Kosofsky Sedgwick (1950–2009) and Adrienne Rich (1929–2012). You might wish to research their ideas using the internet and see how far you think they might be applied to *Streetcar* and the other texts you are studying for A-level. In particular, you might use the critical lens of queer theory to analyse Williams' portrayal of Blanche's tragic husband Allan Grey. What does his fate suggest about public attitudes to homosexuality at the time the play was written?

Performance criticism

Performance criticism looks at how the form of dramatic texts is determined by their basis in theatrical practice, examining them against what is known of the original stage conditions for which they were produced and the way they have been represented subsequently in other theatres and performance media. The approach looks at the essential elements of drama such as words, movement, sound, costume, setting and staging, and questions the notion of a definitive version of a dramatic text, given that theatre is an essentially collaborative and ephemeral medium.

Streetcar has always been seen as one of Williams' masterworks, if not the best thing he ever did. As Felicia Hardison Londré has noted, there is no doubt about 'the centrality of *A Streetcar Named Desire* in his dramatic canon as well as in the American cultural consciousness'. She continues:

> *Whether or not* A Streetcar Named Desire *is Tennessee Williams' 'best' play, or even his most performed play, it is probably the one most closely associated with the dramatist, and it is certainly the one that has elicited the most critical commentary.*

> Londré in Roudané, 1997

In his own lifetime, among the major stars closely associated with Williams' work on stage and screen were Academy Award-winning Hollywood greats such as Marlon Brando, Vivien Leigh, Katharine Hepburn, Paul Newman and Elizabeth Taylor; their eagerness to work with him strongly suggests that his plays were seen to offer immense challenges and possibilities in performance terms. Arguably the symbiosis between Williams and these major actors suggests he had a significant impact on American cinema as well as upon the American stage. Moreover, even three decades after his death it seems his plays can still sprinkle their stardust across a new generation of actors. The 2009 Donmar Warehouse production of *Streetcar* was enthusiastically received, with Rachel Weisz's Blanche being described by theatre critic Henry Hitchings in *the Evening Standard* as:

> *Cleopatra by way of Miss Havisham, deliberately constructing a succession of roles (or disguises) for herself in order to keep reality at bay in a play which dramatises the tension between dark male impulses and feminine poise ... [and] shows as well how vulgarity can bludgeon finer feelings into submission. Above all, it limns [paints] the destructiveness of desire. Blanche arrives on a streetcar at the cramped apartment in Elysian Fields that her sister Stella shares with Stanley. The vehicle's name, Desire, appears a symptom of the city's viscous sensuality, and the 'collapsible' bed in which she is expected to sleep symbolises the intriguingly uncertain social and sexual boundaries of her world – which are soon aggressively policed by Stanley.*

Rachel Weisz received the Laurence Olivier Award for Best Actress for her performance, with Ruth Wilson named Best Supporting Actress for her role as Stella. Five years later, Gillian Anderson received equally glowing reviews for her performance in the Young Vic production, taking home the Evening Standard Award for Best Actress of 2014. *The Telegraph*'s Charles Spencer wrote of this stage interpretation:

> *I staggered out of this shattering production of Tennessee Williams' bruising modern classic feeling shaken, stirred and close to tears.*

Never have I seen a production of the play that was so raw in its emotion, so violent and so deeply upsetting.

First staged in 1947, the piece is usually staged in the period in which it was written.

The iconoclastic director Benedict Andrews is having none of that. The action is set in present day New Orleans, with great blasts of tumultuous rock music by the likes of Jimi Hendrix and Chris Isaak.

The staging is equally compelling, with all the action taking place in a sleek modern apartment, which revolves almost constantly throughout the play so that our view of what's happening keeps taking on fresh perspectives. We see everything from the kitchen to the lavatory in this cramped flat where resentments simmer in the New Orleans heat until they boil over in rage, terror, guilt and mental breakdown. All this might sound like a tricksy directorial ego trip but the effect is to make us see a familiar play with fresh eyes, as if we are experiencing it for the first time. We often stage Shakespeare in modern dress, Andrews seems to be saying. Why not Tennessee Williams too?

The acting is superb, with Gillian Anderson giving the performance of her career as Blanche DuBois, the faded Southern belle of a big Mississippi mansion who has lost her home before the action begins and loses her mind by play's end.

Petite and vulnerable, she captures the syrupy southern charm of the woman which so provokes her blue-collar brother-in-law Stanley Kowalski, and you readily understand why he finds her affected ways so infuriating. But as the play progresses, Anderson devastatingly captures a woman whose options are running out and who is getting ever closer to the end of her rope. Suddenly her lies and fantasies of a better life seem almost heroic, and her final crack-up is almost too painful to watch.

Ben Foster, sweaty, burly and impressively tattooed, brings a thrilling edge of violence to the stage as Kowalski, while Vanessa Kirby as his wife Stella is poignantly torn between her husband and her sister. Nor does she leave any doubt that it is in part her husband's violence that attracts her. This is not a view that goes down well these days and it is part of the courage of both the play and the production that this issue isn't shirked.

The show lasts three and a half hours, but there isn't a moment when the tension slackens or attention lapses. It is an absolute knock-out.

Context

In 1995 the composer and conductor André Previn wrote an opera based on *Streetcar* for which Philip Littell provided the lyrics. In his 2004 article 'The Media are Stepping on Our Toes' Jacques Coulardeau compares the original play with the 1951 film and the Previn/Littell opera and discusses the distinctive features of each genre. You can download a pdf of this article at: www.cercles.com/n10/coulardeau.pdf

CRITICAL VIEW

Carry out an internet search for some other reviews of the 2014 Young Vic stage production to compare with Charles Spencer's and see how far the critics' responses tap into your own ideas about the play. If you were directing a production of *Streetcar*, would you set it in 1947, when it was written, or choose to bring it right up to date, as in the 2014 Young Vic version? Give reasons for your decision. You can find Charles Spencer's review on the Telegraph online (the web address can be found on page 106).

▲ Gillian Anderson as Blanche in the Young Vic 2014 stage production of *A Streetcar Named Desire*

Working with the text

Assessment Objectives and skills

> **AO1** Articulate informed, personal and creative responses to literary texts, using associated concepts and terminology, and coherent, accurate written expression.

To do well with AO1 you need to write fluently, structuring your essay carefully, guiding your reader clearly through your line of argument and using the sophisticated vocabulary, including critical terminology, which is appropriate to an A-level essay. You will need to use frequent embedded quotations to show detailed knowledge and demonstrate familiarity with the whole text. Your aim is to produce a well written academic essay employing appropriate discourse markers to create the sense of a shaped argument; it should use sophisticated terminology at times while remaining clear and cohesive.

> **AO2** Analyse ways in which meanings are shaped in literary texts.

Strong students do not work only on a lexical level, but write well on the generic and structural elements of the play, so it is useful to start by analysing those larger elements of narrative organisation before considering Williams' language. If 'form is meaning', what are the implications of categorising the play as an American tragedy as opposed to a melodrama? The play is structured in a very distinctive way; think about Williams' decision to present 11 scenes as opposed to two or three acts. Then again, to discuss language in detail you will need to quote from the text, analyse that quotation and use it to illuminate your argument. Moreover, since you will at times need to make points about larger generic and organisational features of the text that are much too long to quote, being able to reference effectively is just as important as mastering the art of the embedded quotation. Practise writing in analytical sentences, comprising a brief quotation or close reference, a definition or description of the feature you intend to analyse, an explanation of how this feature has been used and an evaluation of its effectiveness.

> **AO3** Demonstrate understanding of the significance and influence of the contexts in which literary texts are written and received.

To access AO3 successfully you need to think about how contexts of production, reception, literature, culture, biography, geography, society, history, genre and intertextuality can affect texts. Place the play at the heart of the web of contextual factors which you feel have had the most impact upon it; examiners want to see a sense of contextual alertness woven seamlessly into the fabric of your essay rather than a clumsy bolted-on website rehash or some recycled history notes. Show you understand that literary works contain encoded representations of the cultural, moral, religious, racial and political values of the society from which they emerged, and that over time attitudes and ideas change until the views they reflect are no longer widely shared.

A04	Explore connections across literary texts.

If your examination board requires you to compare and contrast one or more other texts with *A Streetcar Named Desire* you must try to find specific points of comparison, rather than merely generalising. You will find it easier to make connections between texts (of any kind) if you try to balance them as you write; remember also that connections are not only about finding similarities – differences are just as interesting. Above all, consider how the comparison illuminates each text; some connections will be thematic, others generic or stylistic.

A05	Explore literary texts informed by different interpretations.

For A05, you should refer to the opinions of critics and remain alert to aspects of the novel which are open to interpretation. Your job is to measure your own interpretation of the text against those of other readers. As a text that has generated widely differing responses, *Streetcar* lends itself readily to the range of interpretations which have been noted in the 'Critical approaches' section of this book (pages 76–84 of this guide). Try to convey an awareness of multiple readings as well as an understanding that (as Barthes suggested) the play's meaning is dependent as much upon what you bring to it as what Williams left there. Using modal verb phrases such as 'may be seen as', 'might be interpreted as' or 'could be represented as' shows you know that different readers interpret texts in different ways at different times. The key word here is plurality; there is no single meaning or one right answer. Relish getting your teeth into the views of published critics to push forward your own argument, but always keep in mind that meanings in texts are shifting and unstable as opposed to fixed and permanent.

Summary

Overall, the hallmarks of a successful A-level essay that hits all five AOs include:

▼ a clear introduction which orientates the reader and outlines your main argument

▼ a coherent and conceptualised argument which relates to the question title

▼ confident movement around the text rather than a relentless chronological trawl through it

- apt and effective quotations or references adapted to make sense within the context of your own sentence
- a range of effective points about Williams' dramatic methods
- a strong and personally engaged awareness of how a text can be interpreted by different readers and audiences in different ways at different times
- a sense that you are prepared to take on a good range of critical and theoretical perspectives
- a conclusion which effectively summarises and consolidates your response and relates it back to your essay title.

Building skills 1: Structuring your writing

This Building skills section focuses upon organising your written responses to convey your ideas as clearly and effectively as possible: the 'how' of your writing as opposed to the 'what'. More often than not, if your knowledge and understanding of *A Streetcar Named Desire* is sound, a disappointing mark or grade will be down to one of two common mistakes: misreading the question or failing to organise your response economically and effectively. In an examination you'll be lucky if you can demonstrate 5 per cent of what you know about *Streetcar*; luckily, if it's the right 5 per cent, that's all you need to gain full marks.

Understanding your examination

It's important to prepare for the specific type of response your examination body sets with regard to *A Streetcar Named Desire*. You'll almost certainly know whether you are studying the play as part of a **non-examined assessment unit** (i.e. for coursework) or as an **examination set text** – but you also need to know if your paper is **Open Book** – i.e. you will have a clean copy of the text available to you in the exam, or **Closed Book**, in which case you won't. You must find out about this, because the format of your assessment has major implications for the way you organise your response and dictates the depth and detail required to achieve a top band mark.

Open Book

In an Open Book exam when you have a copy of *Streetcar* on the desk in front of you, there can be no possible excuse for failing to quote relevantly, accurately and extensively. To gain a high mark, you are expected to focus in detail on specific passages. Remember, too, that you must not refer to any supporting material such as the Introduction Notes contained within the set edition of your text. If an examiner suspects that you have been lifting chunks of unacknowledged material from such a source, they will refer your paper to the examining body for possible plagiarism.

Closed Book

In a Closed Book exam, because the examiner is well aware that you do not have your text in front of you, their expectations will be different. While you are still expected to support your argument with relevant quotations, close textual references are also encouraged and rewarded. Again, since you will have had to memorise quotations, slight inaccuracies will not be severely punished. Rather than a forensically detailed analysis of a specific section of *Streetcar*, the examiner will expect you to range more broadly across the play to structure your response.

Non-examined assessment (NEA)

Writing about *Streetcar* within a non-examined assessment unit (i.e. coursework) context poses a very different set of challenges from an examination in that incorrect quotations and disorientating arguments are liable to cost you much more dearly. Your essay must be wholly and consistently relevant to the title selected; there's no excuse for going off track if you or your teacher mapped out the parameters of your chosen topic in the first place.

Step 1: Planning and beginning: locate the debate

A very common type of exam question invites you to open up a debate about the text by using various trigger words and phrases such as **'consider the view that …'**, **'some readers think that …'** or **'how far do you agree with this view?'** When analysing this type of question, the one thing you can be sure of is that exam questions never offer a view that makes no sense at all or one so blindingly obvious all anyone can do is agree with it; there will always be a genuine interpretation at stake. Similarly many NEA tasks are written to include a stated view to help give some shape to your writing, so logically your introduction needs to address the terms of this debate and sketch out the outlines of how you intend to move the argument forward to orientate the reader. Since it's obviously going to be helpful if you actually know this before you start writing, you really do need to plan before you begin to write.

Undertaking a lively debate about some of the ways in which *Streetcar* has been and can be interpreted is the DNA of your essay. Of course any good argument needs to be honest but to begin by writing 'yes, I totally agree with this obviously true statement' suggests a fundamental misunderstanding of what studying literature is all about. Any stated view in an examination question is designed to open up critical conversations, not shut them down.

Plan your answer by collecting together points for and against the given view. Aim to see a stated opinion as an interesting way of focusing upon a key facet of *Streetcar*, like the following student.

Student A

This student is answering a sample examination task that works with a given view. The question, which is clearly designed to open up a debate, is:

'*A Streetcar Named Desire* is loosely structured and initially takes a lot of time to get going before rushing through its final scenes at a breathless pace.'
To what extent do you agree with this view?

While *A Streetcar Named Desire* (1947) may indeed be seen to have quite a loosely structured timeframe, I think it is significant that Williams claimed his other great play *Cat on a Hot Tin Roof* (1955) came 'closest to being both a work of art and a work of craft'. He described it in his *Memoirs* as 'really very well put together ... it adheres to the valuable edict of Aristotle that a tragedy must have unity of time and place and magnitude of theme'. Strongly contrasting with *Cat on a Hot Tin Roof*'s 'perfect' classical structure, in which all the events take place in real time on one evening, the more loosely structured dramatic action in *Streetcar* unfolds gradually between May to October in a way that seems much more modern and free-flowing to me. The audience senses Blanche's overstayed welcome and the claustrophobic New Orleans summer building up over time in the first half of the play, before a quick sequence of scenes set on Blanche's birthday result in a shocking dramatic climax as first Mitch fails to visit, next Stella goes into labour, then Mitch attacks Blanche and finally is raped by Stanley.

Examiner's commentary

This student:

❧ selects one significant point of connection to develop in detail, using Williams' own ideas about *Cat on a Hot Tin Roof* to evaluate and extend her response to the given view

❧ knows that all quotations – whether from *Streetcar* or a secondary source – are included within the word limit for the NEA unit, so splices in neatly modified quotations that fit with her own syntax

❧ comments meaningfully on AO2 by connecting the contrasting methods used in the two plays

❧ uses Williams' own view of his work as a benchmark to calibrate her personal response to each text

❧ expresses a confident and original personal view that conveys the sense that she has grasped the 'big picture' by arguing that despite the technical perfection of *Cat*, in her opinion *Streetcar*'s 'modern and free-flowing' structure provides greater excitement, interest and tension for the audience.

If the rest of her essay reached this level of performance, it is likely she would be on course to achieve a notional grade A.

Step 2: Developing and linking: go with the flow

An essay is a very specific type of formal writing that requires an appropriate discourse structure. In the main body of your writing, you need to thread your developing argument through each paragraph consistently and logically, referring back to the terms established by the question itself, rephrasing and reframing as you go. It can be challenging to sustain the flow of your essay and keep firmly on track, but here are some techniques to help you.

◥ Ensure your essay doesn't disintegrate into a series of disconnected building blocks by creating a neat and stable bridge between one paragraph and the next.

◥ Use discourse markers – linking words and phrases like 'on the other hand', 'however', 'although' and 'moreover' – to hold the individual paragraphs of your essay together and signpost the connections between different sections of your overarching argument.

◥ Having set out an idea in paragraph A, in paragraph B you might need to then support it by providing a further example; if so, signal this to the reader with a phrase such as *'Moreover, this imagery of white light can also be seen when ...'.*

◥ To change direction and challenge an idea begun in paragraph A by acknowledging that it is open to interpretation, you could begin paragraph B with something like *'On the other hand, this view of the play could be challenged by a feminist critic ...'.*

◥ Another typical paragraph-to-paragraph link is when you want to show that the original idea doesn't give the full picture. Here you could modify your original point with something like *'Although it is possible to see Blanche's remarks about Stanley and his working-class friends as snobbish and even racist, this view does not take account of the social context of the 1940s, when her comments would have seemed much less offensive.'*

Student B

This is another student's essay, answering the same question as Student A:

'*A Streetcar Named Desire* is loosely structured and initially takes a lot of time to get going before rushing through its final scenes at a breathless pace.'
To what extent do you agree with this view?

A Streetcar Named Desire is divided into a string of eleven scenes evoking the images of pearls of a necklace. This unconventional structure builds and sustains dramatic tension partly through the way in which each scene ends with a moment of dramatic intensity such as Blanche's cry at the end of Scene 1 'I'm going to be sick!' I believe the cumulative effect of these tableaux gives the play a cinematic quality which is not surprising, considering Williams lived through the Golden Age of Hollywood.

As well as the episodic modern structure, however, Williams also incorporates elements of classical Greek tragedy in abiding to some extent by Aristotle's unities. The unity of place is clear – all the action takes place in the Kowalskis' apartment – as is the unity of action, in that the play is purely centred on Blanche, Stanley, Stella and Mitch with no sub-plots. Moreover, I would argue that Williams' decision to ignore the unity of time highlights his interest in prolonging claustrophobic tension and allowing for deeper character development, as cramming all the intense dramatic action into a period of, say, twenty-four hours could render the play superficial and unconvincing.

Examiner's commentary

This student:

- expresses her ideas with flair and imagination – the image of *Streetcar*'s individual scenes resembling the 'pearls of a necklace' is vivid and original, as well as accurate
- creates very good cohesion between paragraphs by clearly connecting the stages of her argument
- uses well-chosen discourse markers – 'as well as', ' however', 'also' and 'moreover' – to signpost the flow of her ideas
- makes a very neat paragraph-to-paragraph link to indicate that the point made in the first section doesn't give the full picture; the student argues cogently that the play's structure is not just modern and cinematic, but also classically tragic in some respects.

If the rest of her essay reached this level of performance, it is likely she would be on course to achieve a notional grade A.

Step 3: Concluding: seal the deal

As you bring your writing to a close, you need to capture and clarify your response to the given view and make a relatively swift and elegant exit. Keep your final paragraph short and sweet. Now is not the time to introduce any new points – but equally, don't just reword everything you have already just said either. Neat potential closers include:

- looping the last paragraph back to something you mentioned in your introduction to suggest that you have now said all there is to say on the subject

> ◄ reflecting on your key points in order to reach a balanced overview

> ◄ ending with a punchy quotation that leaves the reader thinking

> ◄ discussing the contextual implications of the topic you have debated

> ◄ reversing expectations to end on an interesting alternative view

> ◄ stating why you think the main issue, theme or character under discussion is so central to the play

> ◄ mentioning how different audiences over time might have responded to the topic you have been debating.

Student C

Like Students A and B, this student is also working to answer the same question:

'A Streetcar Named Desire is loosely structured and initially takes a lot of time to get going before rushing through its final scenes at a breathless pace.' To what extent do you agree with this view?

Remember to include relevant detailed exploration of Williams' authorial methods in your answer.

Overall it is so true that the book is loosely structured. I think this is shown very well in the scene where Blanche, Stanley and Stella are having tea on Blanche's birthday. Williams uses dramatic tension because for Stanley this is his best scene, he is finally getting the revenge on Blanche he has been waiting for. Throughout the book it has been a constant battle between them, they have been rivals from the beginning and now we see him getting the upper hand at last. We get to see how cruel he is, his mission is to destroy her and he picks the perfect time, her birthday. As the play enters the last sections, we begin to see the destruction of Blanche; she seems almost to crumble before the reader's eyes like the paper lantern that Stanley destroys. Williams used the metaphor of white light to describe Blanche before and the birthday is significant as she has always been hyper-sensitive about her age, however she seems so wrapped up in the fact Mitch isn't there that our attention goes to Stanley and he takes control. This really sets the scene for what is going to happen in the final part of the play. However, the last scene is much later than the night of the birthday party which could be detached and confusing, so overall I do mainly agree that Streetcar is loosely structured.

Examiner's commentary

This student:

▼ accepts rather uncritically the given view that the play is loosely structured and (as seen in the last sentence) that this is some kind of mistake or problem

▼ fails to finish by clarifying his argument or actively debating the original task focus

▼ takes the tried-and-tested route of *partially* accepting the stated view to some extent but does not challenge it very effectively

▼ labels the technical term 'dramatic tension' but fails to identify a clear example of the technique as used by Williams or analyse its effects

▼ includes some feature-spotting with the statement that 'Williams uses the metaphor of white light to describe Blanche' since there is no analysis of how or why the playwright does this.

If the rest of his essay reached this level of performance, it is likely he would be on course to achieve a notional grade C/D.

Building skills 2: Analysing texts in detail

Having worked through the Building skills section 1: Structuring your writing, this section of the guide contains a range of annotated extracts from students' responses to *A Streetcar Named Desire*. The next few pages will enable you to assess the extent to which these students have successfully demonstrated their writing skills and mastery of the Assessment Objectives to provide you with an index by which to measure your own skills progress. Each extract comes with a commentary to help you identify what each student is doing well and/or what changes they would need to make to their writing to target a higher grade.

The main focus here is on the ways in which you can successfully include within your own well-structured writing clear and appropriate references to both *Streetcar* itself and the ways in which other readers have responded to the play. In an examination, of course, the 'other reading' you need to refer to consistently is the one expressed in the question itself. In a non-examined assessment unit, you will have more choice about which interpretations of the text you most want to work with – but since you have much more time and may well have written your own question title, you have even less excuse to wander off task.

Analysis in examination tasks

Student A

This student is answering an examination task which puts forward a specific view. The question, which is clearly designed to open up a debate, is:

'First and foremost this play is about a clash between two cultures.'

Examine this view of *A Streetcar Named Desire*.

One of the ways in which Williams may be seen to present a culture clash is through using binary oppositions to interpret the specific context of the postwar American South. The playwright links the political/cultural dimension with the personal/individual aspect through the violent confrontation of Blanche and Stanley, and hints at this from the start through their contrasting clothing; whereas she is 'daintily dressed in a white suit' he is 'roughly dressed in blue denim work clothes'. Williams dramatically juxtaposes their cultural heritages, as she embodies the Old South whereas he represents a second generation immigrant community whose values and customs are the total opposite of hers.

Another way in which Williams chooses to emphasise the culture clash in *Streetcar* is by bringing together two individuals fated to become deadly enemies. In fact Stanley senses straight away that Blanche poses a real threat to him; when she says she comes from Laurel, Mississippi, he dismisses it as not 'my 'territory'. Blanche, like the Old South, is vulnerable, trapped by the values of a crumbling conservative aristocracy that will be crushed by the more liberal and energetic postwar world Stanley represents. Moreover, from the very beginning of the play Williams can be seen to employ the classic 'arrival of the stranger' scenario to set up dramatic tension and his metaphorical stage direction likening Blanche to an uncertain 'moth' suggests that someone this fragile will inevitably struggle to sustain her identity within the cultural environment of the Quarter.

Examiner's commentary

This student:

- ◥ refers back to the terms of the question frequently, reframing the buzzwords 'culture clash' along the way
- ◥ mentions Tennessee Williams as the maker of textual meaning frequently when analysing his stagecraft and themes
- ◥ takes on the premise of the question by suggesting that the playwright has consciously linked the 'political/cultural' and 'personal/individual' aspects of the text – it seems likely that this opinion would be developed further to provide the spine of his essay
- ◥ uses appropriate connectives like 'thus' and 'moreover' to signal the developing stages of his argument
- ◥ forges a very clear link between his two paragraphs that achieves cohesion and thus reassures the examiner that he is still fully on task
- ◥ uses the modal verb phrases 'may be seen to' and 'can be seen to' together with the subtle verb 'suggests' to flag up his awareness that textual meanings are unfixed and always open to question
- ◥ embeds short snippets of quotation within his own sentences seamlessly, so that the flow of his writing is not disrupted

> - quotes frequently and always relevantly – the single well-chosen word 'moth' showcases the student's ability to select the precise term to clinch his point and incorporates this within a sentence that also makes a very good point about dramatic structure
> - demonstrates very good AO2 knowledge in terms of structure by referring to binary opposition.
>
> **If the rest of his examination answer reached this level of performance, it is likely he would be on course to achieve a notional grade A.**

Student B

This student is answering an examination task which works with a given view. The question, which is clearly designed to open up a debate, is:

How far do you agree that *A Streetcar Named Desire* fails because the relationship between Stella and Stanley is totally unconvincing?

Stella gave up her Southern family, their social status and traditional values in order to marry the charming ex-soldier Stanley Kowalski. He, however, is an American who originated from Poland. He is a mechanic, and a powerful character in his group of friends which he is definitely in control of. Stanley is the alpha male type. His relationship with Stella is quite extreme in some ways as their relationship is mostly based on sex alone. His rugged looks are most definitely what drew Stella to him compared to her previous upper class lifestyle. You can see in Stella's reaction to Blanche's sarcastic comments that she is happy living the working class life, she says 'Don't you think your superior attitude is a bit out of place here?' Williams shows how Stanley made her change her life entirely and Stella is drawn in. It's like an obsession she has no control over. Their relationship is up and down with fierce passion intensified by the hot summer weather. The weather gives a real sense of the big change of moods, the two don't care much for their belongings or the appearance of things and have a basic way of living. This can be seen by Eunice's reaction to Blanche's expressions as she sets eyes on the flat for the first time. '[defensively, noticing Blanche's look]: It's sort of messed up right now but when it's clean it's real sweet.' The use of lighting and the focus on the apartment where the main events happen shows the setting is important.

▼ fails to unpick the terms of the given view of Stanley and Stella's relationship – i.e. whether it is or isn't fundamentally unbelievable to the point where it undermines the play

▼ fails to make the central premise of the question central to her argument or sustain any sense of a debate about the interpretation stated

▼ shifts midway through this long paragraph from a discussion of the pathetic fallacy – which was quite promising in signalling some AO2 at last – to the state of the Kowalskis' flat and the play's setting in a rather abrupt and disorientating manner without a paragraph break

▼ makes some statements which are very much open to question, or at the very least require further explanation, such as describing Stanley as 'charming' or that he 'originated from Poland' when he is 'proud as hell' of having been born in the USA

▼ writes for a long time before using any direct quotations at all before introducing them to prove points only, rather than analysing their language effects

▼ does address AO2 towards the end of the paragraph by writing about setting, but without linking these points effectively to the central viewpoint embedded within the question.

If the rest of her examination answer reached this level of performance, it is likely she would be on course to achieve a notional grade C/D.

Analysis in non-examined assessments

Student A

In this extract from a sample examination task from AQA Specification B, Section B, the student is answering the following question:

Write about the presentation of relationships by three writers you have studied.

In this section of their answer, the student has chosen to compare the relationship of Stanley and Stella from *A Streetcar Named Desire* with that of Demetrius and Helena in Shakespeare's *A Midsummer Night's Dream*. They treated a third text later in their answer.

In issuing the command 'I love thee not, therefore pursue me not,' Demetrius takes on a similar dominant and authoritarian male persona to Stanley, who labels himself a literal ruler of supreme importance; 'I'm the king around here, and don't you forget it.' Furthermore, it might be suggested that Helena's dialogue is so demeaning at times that a modern audience with even a moderately feminist viewpoint may be horrified to hear a woman willingly reduce herself to the level of an abused animal: 'I am your spaniel, and, Demetrius, / The more you beat me, I will fawn on you … spurn me, strike me, / Neglect me, lose me; only give me leave, / Unworthy as I am, to follow you.' I believe that Shakespeare's presentation of a woman abasing herself in order to regain a man's love can be compared and contrasted with Stella's choosing to forgive Stanley after he beats her in a drunken rage. Despite Eunice's disgust and Blanche's horror, it is possible to argue that in returning with apparently no regrets, Stella actually shows her power over Stanley, who sobs like a child and begs his 'baby' to come back to him by 'baying' in an animalistic manner. Indeed Williams' stage directions describe the couple coming together 'with low animal moans' that signal they will end their quarrel by making love. Significantly, when Blanche tries to persuade her sister to leave Stanley the next morning, Stella declares 'You take it for granted that I'm in something I want to get out of.' This dialogue, together with her remark that the radio Stanley hurled out of the window can be easily fixed – 'only one tube was smashed' – implies that despite the violence, Stella wants the marriage, like the radio, to go on. The fact that Stella 'was sort of thrilled' by Stanley's ferocity on their wedding night, when he smashed up the light bulbs with the heel of her slipper, shows that in this modern tragedy passion and violence are linked in a way that some may find even more disturbing than Helena's self-abasement. After all, since *A Midsummer Night's Dream* is a comedy, Helena's dialogue could be accompanied by an exaggerated, almost slapstick set of actions that take the sting out of her doormat-style dialogue.

Examiner's commentary

Note how this student:

- uses the 'I' voice confidently and clearly to stress her own point of view
- makes very good references to the different ways in which texts have been written and can be received – e.g. by flagging up the different ways in which a contemporary audience and a 'modern feminist' audience might respond to both plays' descriptions of apparently abusive relationships
- uses the modal verb phrases *'it is possible to argue'*, *'it might be suggested'* and *'may be horrified'*, together with the subtle verb 'implies' to flag up the idea of multiple interpretations of text
- signals a very confident awareness of the context of stage performance by mentioning the impact of Stanley's yelling for Stella and then building on this by suggesting a way in which the impact of Helena's behaviour might be presented theatrically to mitigate her 'doormat-style dialogue'
- shapes her essay by ranging across *Streetcar* to find the most useful reference points to support her argument rather than 'going through' the text to the point where the essay feels plodding and 'listy'
- recognises that since there is no way to cover everything within the confines of a tight NEA word limit, she needs to write 'a lot about a little' not 'a little about a lot'
- interweaves *Streetcar* and *A Midsummer Night's Dream* within the same paragraph rather than treating them separately, using the language of connection in 'compared and contrasted' and 'similarity' to signal that she has found patterns of both similarity and difference across the texts
- selects one significant point to develop in detail and clusters her supporting material around this very effectively, referring to stage directions and performance as well as language to access AO2.

If the rest of her examination answer reached this level of performance, it is likely she would be on course to achieve a notional grade A.

Before studying this section, you should identify your own 'top ten' quotations – i.e. those phrases or sentences that seem to capture a key theme or aspect of the text most aptly and memorably – and clearly identify what it is about your choices that makes each one so significant. No two readers of *A Streetcar Named Desire* will select exactly the same set and it will be well worth discussing (and perhaps even having to defend) your choices with the other students in your class.

When you have done this, look carefully at the following list of top ten quotations and consider each one's possible significance within the play. How might each be used in an essay response to support your exploration of various elements or readings of *A Streetcar Named Desire*? Consider what these quotations tell us about Tennessee Williams' ideas, themes and methods as well as how far they may contribute to various potential ways of interpreting the text.

Blanche: They told me to take a street-car named Desire, and then transfer to one called Cemeteries and ride six blocks and get off at – Elysian Fields! (Scene I, page 4)

1

> The central allegorical image of the play is this one of the streetcar which represents those forbidden sexual adventures which have brought Blanche to the land of the dead and represent the diametrically opposed Freudian impulses of eros and thanatos. Her sojourn at the Kowalskis' apartment will prove a sort of staging post in her journey towards that death-in-life in the asylum which is connoted by the end of the streetcar line – Cemeteries.

Blanche: There are thousands of papers, stretching back over hundreds of years, affecting Belle Reve as, piece by piece, our improvident grandfathers and father and uncles and brothers exchanged the land for their epic fornications – to put it plainly!…The four-letter word deprived us of our plantation, till finally all that was left – and Stella can verify that! – was the house itself and about twenty acres of ground, including a graveyard, to which now all but Stella and I have retreated. (Scene II, page 22)

2

> Blanche's speech for the defence after Stanley accuses her of having cheated Stella lays the blame for the loss of Belle Reve squarely on their corrupt DuBois ancestors, but this only serves to stress that she is their direct heir in sexual as well as economic terms. Morally as well as financially bankrupt, Blanche represents the moribund Southern aristocracy who are utterly irrelevant in the new post-war world.

3

Mitch: Could it be – you and me, Blanche? (Scene VI, page 57)

Mitch's touching proposal springs from the one time Blanche tells him the truth about her past and reveals the story of Allan Grey's suicide; his offer represents her last hope of finding someone to look after her. While she would never have seen the lumbering working-class Mitch as a suitable beau in her heyday, in her present circumstances Blanche recognises that he could offer her a lifeline. Ironically what causes him to abandon her may be her lies rather than her promiscuity, because when Stanley tells him about Blanche's past, Mitch feels she has made a fool of him.

4

Stanley: I am not a Polack. People from Poland are Poles, not Polacks. But what I am is one hundred per cent American, born and raised in the greatest country on earth and proud as hell of it, so don't ever call me a Polack. (Scene VIII, page 67)

As Blanche once again drops one of her unpleasant social clangers, Stanley attracts our sympathy, coming across as an all-American hero, forcefully (and rather magnificently) declaring that he is a son of Uncle Sam to his fingertips. The Old South she represents is dead in the water, while active, hardworking new Americans are popping up to claim their own piece of the American Dream.

5

Stanley: When we first met, me and you, you thought I was common. How right you was, baby. I was common as dirt. You showed me the snapshot of the place with the columns. I pulled you down off them columns and how you loved it, having them coloured lights going! And wasn't we happy together, wasn't it all okay till she showed here? (Scene VIII, page 68)

This quotation shows that, like Blanche, Stanley too has a public life and a private inner life which is comprised of intimate memories, dreams and desires. The coloured lights represent the passion between Stanley and Stella which persuaded her to abandon her aristocratic past and build a future with him in New Orleans. Unlike the cold white marble pillars of Belle Reve, apparently the setting for a Greek tragedy, Stanley's 'coloured lights' are vibrant and vivid. Whereas Blanche often wears white – this is what her name means – Stanley wears gaudy bowling shirts and bright silk pyjamas. This speech thus encapsulates Stella's dilemma, caught between the past and the future.

6

Stanley: I've been on to you from the start! Not once did you pull any wool over this boy's eyes! You come in here and sprinkle the place with powder and spray perfume and cover the light-bulb with a paper lantern, and lo and behold the place has turned into Egypt and you are the Queen of the Nile! Sitting on your throne and swilling down my liquor! I say – *Ha-Ha!* Do you hear me? *Ha-ha-ha!* (Scene X, page 79)

> This is another of the play's frequent metatheatrical references to acting and performance, as Stanley brutally strips away the pathetic remnants of Blanche's dignity. Having previously referred to her putting on 'her act' (page 60), here he reveals his awareness of the gulf between her constant masquerades and poses and the ugly truth beneath, and mercilessly he brings her shaky house of cards tumbling down. Moreover, in mocking her as a dime-store Cleopatra, Stanley's speech also foreshadows her eventual tragic downfall.

7

Stanley: We've had this date with each other from the beginning! (Scene X, page 81)

> Stanley's words here suggest that Blanche's fate has been decided all along, and that the powerful sexual tension which has constantly arced between them is about to short-circuit at the climax of the play. The line jars slightly with what has come before it, as the dialogue between Stanley and Blanche appears to allow for the possibility that they have once again misunderstood one another, and that the rape was not in fact premeditated; thus its inclusion surely suggests that Blanche's downfall was inevitable, and all of a piece with Stanley's ominous remark to Stella in Scene VII, 'Her future is mapped out for her' (page 63).

8

Eunice: Don't ever believe it. Life has got to go on. No matter what happens, you've got to keep on going. (Scene XI, page 83)

> Eunice's words to Stella encapsulate her working-class gut instinct for survival and authorise her friend's decision to abandon Blanche to her fate in order to go on living with Stanley. In the dog-eat-dog world of the new post-war America, Eunice knows that Stella has to put her love for her baby, her need for economic protection and the future of her marriage above her loyalty to her sister and her past, even if her feelings for Stanley are fatally compromised.

Blanche: … I have always depended on the kindness of strangers. (Scene XI, page 89)

Blanche's final words show that she has finally abandoned the real world for her fantasy life and reimagines the doctor who has come to take her to the asylum as the chivalrous beau (personified by Shep Huntleigh) by whom she longs to be rescued. Ironically it was her constant search for love and support – 'the kindness of strangers' – which led her to her ruin in the first place, although she seems to have accepted that she has no one else to turn to now Stella has deserted her. Several 'strangers' appear to Blanche during the play – the Young Man, the Mexican Woman, the Negro Woman and the Prostitute – and each encounter seems to leave her more isolated and vulnerable than the last.

Steve: This game is seven-card stud. (Scene XI, page 90)

As the men pick up the threads of their poker game after Blanche has been taken away to the asylum, Steve's words suggest that the game of life as played in the new America is one whose rules are laid down by – and serve to benefit – brutal men rather than vulnerable women. In this context, perhaps Stella's decision to stand by her man may seem the only sensible one she could make.

Taking it further

Books

▼ Bigsby, C. (2000) *Modern American Drama, 1945–2000*, Cambridge University Press
  – An excellent overview of twentieth-century drama with much to say about other playwrights such as Arthur Miller, this book contains an interesting chapter called 'Tennessee Williams: the Theatricalising Self'. Selected extracts can be viewed online via a Google Books search.

▼ McEvoy, S. (2009) *Tragedy: A Student Handbook*, English and Media Centre
  – An excellent introduction to the tragic genre, this book contains a section on modern American tragedy giving an overview of Williams' life and work and discusses *A Streetcar Named Desire*, *Cat on a Hot Tin Roof* and *The Glass Menagerie* in detail.

▼ Roudané, M. (ed.) (1997) *The Cambridge Companion to Tennessee Williams*, Cambridge University Press
  – A superb collection of articles including Felicia Hardison Londré's 'A Streetcar Running Fifty Years'; Nancy M. Tischler's 'Romantic textures in Tennessee Williams' plays and short stories'; Gilbert Debusscher's 'Creative rewriting: European and American influences on the dramas of Tennessee Williams'; R. Barton Palmer's 'Hollywood in crisis'.

▼ Smith-Howard, A. and Heintzelman, G. (2005) *Critical Companion to Tennessee Williams: A literary reference to his life and work*, Checkmark Books
  – A Williams encyclopaedia, full of stimulating material.

▼ Williams, T. (ed. Margaret Bradham Thornton) (2006) *Notebooks*, Yale University Press
  – A scrapbook mix of diary, biography and autobiography.

▼ Williams, T. (1976) *Cat on a Hot Tin Roof and Other Plays*, Penguin
  – This collection includes Williams' fascinating essay 'Person-to-Person'.

▼ Williams, T. (1976) *Memoirs*, W.H. Allen
  – An absorbing autobiography covering many important aspects of Williams' life and work.

▼ Williams, T. (eds Patricia Hern and Michael Hooper) (1947) *A Streetcar Named Desire*, Methuen Student Edition 2008
  – An excellent edition of the text with a useful introduction and comprehensive glossary.

Weblinks

⇥ Small. R.C. (2004) 'A Teacher's Guide to the Signet edition of Tennessee Williams' *A Streetcar Named Desire*' at:
http://us.penguingroup.com/static/pdf/teachersguides/streetcar.pdf

⇥ The opening scene of *Gone with the Wind* can be found at:
www.youtube.com/watch?v=pL2yPFxBQQ4

⇥ Charles Spencer's review of the 2014 Young Vic production of *A Streetcar Named Desire* can be found at:
www.telegraph.co.uk/news/celebritynews/11264049/Gillian-Anderson-wins-best-actress-for-raw-Blanche-Dubois.html

Films

⇥ **1951:** directed by Elia Kazan – Tennessee Williams was closely associated with this film, the best-known interpretation, but try to look at other available versions too (see below).

⇥ **1984:** directed by John Erman – with Treat Williams as Stanley and Ann-Margret as Blanche.

⇥ **1995:** directed by Glenn Jordan – with Alec Baldwin as Stanley and Jessica Lange as Blanche.